PENGUIN BOOKS

THE WORKING MOTHER'S GUILT GUIDE

Mary C. Hickey is a Washington, D.C.-based free-lance writer and mother of two young children. Her work appears regularly in numerous national magazines and newspapers. Previously, she worked for *The Miami Herald* and for NBC News.

Sandra Salmans is a Philadelphia-based free-lance writer and mother of two young children. She has written for a number of national magazines. Previously, she was a writer for *Newsweek* and a reporter for *The New York Times*.

The
WORKING MOTHER'S
Guilt Guide

Whatever You're Doing,
It Isn't Enough

MARY C. HICKEY AND
SANDRA SALMANS

Illustrated by Charles Beyl

PENGUIN
BOOKS

PENGUIN BOOKS
Published by the Penguin Group
Viking Penguin, a division of Penguin Books USA Inc.,
375 Hudson Street, New York, New York 10014, U.S.A.
Penguin Books Ltd, 27 Wrights Lane,
London W8 5TZ, England
Penguin Books Australia Ltd, Ringwood,
Victoria, Australia
Penguin Books Canada Ltd, 10 Alcorn Avenue, Suite 300,
Toronto, Ontario, Canada M4V 3B2
Penguin Books (N.Z.) Ltd, 182–190 Wairau Road,
Auckland 10, New Zealand

Penguin Books Ltd, Registered Offices:
Harmondsworth, Middlesex, England

First published in Penguin Books 1992

1 3 5 7 9 10 8 6 4 2

AUTHORS' NOTE:
Although the scenarios we present in this book are all too true, the names and characters are fictitious and any resemblance to actual persons is coincidental.

LIBRARY OF CONGRESS CATALOGING IN PUBLICATION DATA
Hickey, Mary Cassandra.
The working mother's guilt guide : whatever you're doing, it isn't
enough / Mary C. Hickey and Sandra Salmans.
p. cm.
ISBN 0 14 01.6624 6
1. Working mothers—Humor. 2. Guilt—Humor. 3. Working mothers—
United States—Humor. I. Salmans, Sandra. II. Title.
HQ759.48.H53 1992
306.874'3—dc20 91-36449

PRINTED IN THE UNITED STATES OF AMERICA

Set in ITC Garamond Light
Designed by Beth Tondreau Design
Illustrations by Charles Beyl

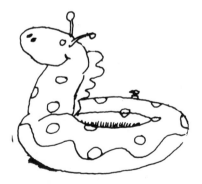

Acknowledgments

To all the Working Mothers who, wittingly and unwittingly, shared their guilt and their humor: Margaret Brown, Anne Bullen, Lydia Chavez, Jane Friedman, Laura Hickey, Rhonda Hudanish, Janet Krop, Cynthia Kuhn, Katie Hickey Lipari, Mary Ryan Manning, Kathleen Mc-Cleery, Desda Moss, Carin Pratt, Marcie Solomon, Susie Stevenson,

Marsha Taubenhaus, Susan Udelson, Patricia Hickey Wlach and, especially, Jane Ottenberg for her careful reading and thoughtful suggestions.

To others for their help and support: Erica Berger, Robin Fried, Peter Sherwood, Dana Smith, Clarice Strasser and Leslie Wayne.

To our Working Mother agent, Gail Ross, and to Mindy Werner at Penguin Books, who became a Working Mother in the course of editing this book. To Janine Steel, also at Penguin.

To Maria Luisa Ramirez and Miriam Avena, who enabled us to work and be mothers at the same time.

To our own mothers, Catherine Hickey and Myrtle Strauss.

And, of course, to our husbands, Fred Strasser and Peter Phillips, without whose contributions we never would have become Working Mothers.

Contents

PART THREE
The Guilt Provokers
Some of the Characters in Our Lives Who Make Us Feel Guilty

PART FOUR
The Guilt Amplifiers
Some Special Situations That Increase Our Guilt

PART FIVE
The Guilt-Free
The All-American Dad

PART SIX
The Guilt Assuagers
Some of the Ridiculous Ways We Cope

Introduction

Congratulations! If you're reading this book, you must be one of the 21.5 million American women who Have It All. Children. A Job. Love and Work.

So what's wrong? Why do you feel that Having It All is too much of a good thing? That whatever you're doing, it isn't enough? That wherever you are, you ought to be someplace else?

Simple. You're probably suffering from Working Mother Guilt.

But just to confirm the diagnosis, take this quick quiz:

It's 8:30 in the morning. You've gotten five-year-old Joshua on the school bus, mopped up a glass of spilled grape juice, stacked the dishwasher and even managed to glance at the front page of the newspaper so you don't look totally surprised when one of your colleagues mentions that the Soviet government has toppled.

But now it's down to the wire. You've got fifteen minutes to find your other earring, hustle the baby off to day-care and get to the office for a Very Important Meeting. Suddenly you notice that little Nora, wearing only her diaper, has a suspicious rash on her chest. It could be chicken pox.

What do you do?

A. Rush toward the poor thing, pick her up, comfort her and talk to her about her boo-boo as you check its appearance against a description in Dr. Spock. Phone your office and tell them you won't be in today and maybe not for the rest of the week.

B. Call Dial-a-Granny, the baby-sitting agency you've used in previous emergencies, ask them to send the same kind and loving woman who's come before, and continue getting ready to leave.

C. Figure that Nora's rash is probably nothing more than an allergic reaction to the grape juice she licked off the floor. Bundle her up in overalls and a turtleneck and drop her off at the day-care center. Make a quick escape.

Undoubtedly your answer says a lot about your sensibilities and mothering style. But for all practical purposes, it really doesn't mean a thing because the bottom line is this: No matter what you've chosen, the result is the same. You feel guilty.

If you've chosen:

C. You feel guilty because you're an awful mother who can't even take a day off to comfort a Sick Child and because you may have exposed a half-dozen other toddlers to some dread disease.

B. You feel guilty because the baby-sitting service has sent a Total Stranger who probably has a Criminal Record and who, at the very least, will let Nora swallow the earring you couldn't find. You also feel guilty because Nora, oblivious to the woman's past, is already calling her Mommy as you sail out the door.

A. You feel guilty that you overreacted to a rash that disappeared after five minutes, and, in the process, you've turned Nora into a budding hypochondriac. And you feel guilty because you end up being late for the meeting, where everyone knows your lateness has something to do with the F-word, as in Family.

You may also feel guilty for calling Nora's rash a "boo-boo."

THE point of this little exercise is to prove something you probably already know: Working Mothers have a lot of guilt.

Guilt is as much a part of our lives as the spare Pampers in our pocketbooks or the car-pool schedules in our briefcases. We feel guilty about practically everything:

That we don't spend enough time with our kids for whom we planned so carefully or whom we waited so long to have.

That we no longer devote nearly as much thought and energy to our careers, which ten years ago were practically our exclusive focus, but which now don't seem all that much different from a plain old j-o-b.

That our dresser drawers are more likely to contain nursing bras from Sears than teddies from Victoria's Secret, and that it doesn't matter anyway because, really, we'd rather sleep than have sex.

That, struggle though we might, our homes have come to look less like June and Ward Cleaver's and more like something invaded by the Cat in the Hat.

That our cooking has deteriorated to the point where even convenience foods take too much time, where french fries and ketchup are the main vegetables, and where a hot meal can mean microwaved popcorn.

That we no longer jog to the health club to tone up the muscles under our stretch marks.

That we haven't read the latest best-seller or seen the hottest new movie, and what's more, don't have any idea what they are and probably won't find out until they're both on videotape.

We even feel guilty when we don't feel guilty. After all, everywhere you look the words "guilt" and "working mother" are linked together like "eighties" and "greed" and "Persian" and "Gulf." And that makes us think we're supposed to feel guilty, and if we don't, we must be hard-hearted women who don't deserve to have children.

What's a mother to do?

Let's try another quiz. Fill in the blank.

We could all _____ .

A. Quit our jobs, stay home, surrender our financial independence, jeopardize our hard-earned careers, be frustrated, drive our kids crazy, who knows, maybe even default on the mortgage or, en masse, bring the U.S. economy to its knees.

B. Keep plugging along, adding still more guilt to the load on our already sagging Power Shoulders, damaging our children, neglecting our jobs, and, in general, making life miserable for ourselves and everyone around us.

C. Accept guilt as a part of life in the 1990s, realize that it is an incredible burden we heap upon ourselves and repeat this mantra: "There are Many, Many Correct Ways to Raise Children." (But, just in case, pray that the next generation will not be as self-indulgent as ours, will not spend hours complaining to some therapist about what their mothers did wrong, and will never form an organization called Adult Children of Working Mothers.)

D. All of the Above.

You've probably chosen D, All of the Above. Add to that one more thing we can do about guilt: Laugh it off.

Which is what this book is designed to help you do.

A CONVERSATION WITH THE DEVIL'S ADVOCATE
About Using the Term "Working Mother" . . .

DEVIL'S ADVOCATE: Do you really want to use the term "Working Mother"?

THE AUTHORS: Sure, why not?

DEVIL'S ADVOCATE: Well, don't you think it suggests that mothers who don't have paying jobs are not working? Being a mother is hard work, you know, even if you don't engage in outside employment.

THE AUTHORS: Hmmm, a good point . . .

DEVIL'S ADVOCATE: And besides, don't you think it's a little sexist to use a term like "Working Mother"? You'd never hear anyone talking about a "Working Father," would you?

THE AUTHORS: Hmmm, another good point . . .

DEVIL'S ADVOCATE: So, why don't you come up with another less offensive term?

THE AUTHORS: Okay. (They confer quietly, then:) What do you think of "Women with Children Who Are Gainfully Employed Outside the Home"?

DEVIL'S ADVOCATE: Gimme a break. What is this, a humor book or a sociological dissertation?

THE AUTHORS: Well, we don't want to offend anyone.

DEVIL'S ADVOCATE: You're bound to offend someone.

THE AUTHORS: Hmmmm, a good point . . .

xvii

PART ONE

In the Beginning

CHAPTER 1

Guilt and the Working Mother-to-Be

Guilt begins at conception.

You may not recognize it at first. The feeling often gets lost in the monsoon of sensations that hits you about now: elation, nervousness, excitement, apprehension, anxiety, ambivalence, confusion, fear, worry, fatigue, and the urge to urinate.

But make no mistake. Working Mother Guilt does not wait for the birth of a child.

This may come as a shock. Until now, you probably thought that Working Mothers feel guilty because they don't spend enough time with their kids. And pregnancy ought to be the only time when you really can have it all. You're spending every second, waking and sleeping, with your child. And you still can throw yourself into your job.

But surprise! Working Mother Guilt comes in three zillion varieties, several of which set in just moments after that sperm hooks up with an eager egg.

Let's say, for example, you've been "trying" to have a baby. Maybe you've even been popping a thermometer in your mouth every morning, scheduling sex as if it were a client meeting and subjecting yourself and your sperm donor, er, husband, to countless other indignities. Finally, you think you've done it. You should feel overjoyed, ecstatic, grateful, maternal—right? Wrong! Instead, you're busily calculating your probable due date, desperately afraid it's going to coincide with your next performance review. Suddenly, it occurs to you that maybe you aren't pregnant after all. You're overcome with grief. The result of these conflicting emotions: guilt.

Or let's say you haven't exactly been trying to get pregnant but, obviously, you haven't been trying hard enough not to. You are not particularly happy when you discover you *are* pregnant. (An understatement. You're considering suing your husband for criminal negligence.) All you care about right now is the fact that you're up for a promotion and when your boss (either a man whose wife's "career" consists of being the local hospital's flower lady, or—worse—a forty-year-old single woman who disdainfully calls children "rug rats") finds out you're pregnant, you will immediately be demoted and will spend the rest of your life working for someone younger, less experienced and nowhere near as qualified as you. As you obsess about all this, you're hit by the tragic recognition that your baby is beginning its life with a mother who doesn't really want it. The result: guilt.

Or maybe this is your second child. Your pregnancy stirs up all the guilt feelings you felt the first time around, then doubles them. You worry about having to ask for maternity leave again. You fret about spending even less time with your firstborn, who will be completely shoved aside. You tell yourself you must be crazy because now you've gone off and upset the unbelievably delicate balance you had finally achieved in your Working Mother life.

The variations on these themes are endless. But just as a microscopic embryo is a precursor to a full-blown baby, the ambivalence and confusion one experiences as one progresses from Working Woman to Working Mother-to-Be are precursors to a full-blown case of guilt.

So, you're pregnant!

Congratulations.

And welcome to Working Motherhood!

A MONTH-BY-MONTH GUIDE TO PREGNANCY GUILT

As a working woman, you've learned that the best way to tackle a new job is to do your homework. So as soon as your do-it-yourself pregnancy test confirms that you've done it, you run to the bookstore and load up on texts telling you how to be pregnant.

Some of the authors make the experience sound so glorious that you double-check to make sure they're talking about pregnancy. Others make it sound so gruesome that, had you read them first, you might have waited until medical science allowed you to get your husband pregnant.

But nowhere in these volumes can you find a discussion of what to expect in the way of guilt. So here, for the first time, is a month-by-month guide to the kinds of guilt you experience from conception to birth.

Your First Month—Your fetus is just a dab of protoplasm, but your role in turning this blob into a baby is rather large. Overwhelmed by the realization that if anything goes wrong, it will be entirely YOUR FAULT, you feel guilty for taking two aspirin, drinking a few sips of Chablis and eating one bite of pepperoni pizza, which your friend's obstetrician's receptionist said can cause placenta previa.

Your Second Month—Your baby is the size of the vitamin pill you keep forgetting to take, but already is making sure you know it's there. Your twenty-four-hour-a-day "morning" sickness makes you feel dreadful enough, but it's compounded by guilt that you're spending more time in the rest room than at your desk—and no one even notices.

Your Third Month—Your baby is still tiny enough for you to keep your condition a secret. You feel guilty for telling your colleagues you have a lingering flu, and lying so convincingly that they all make doctors' appointments to see if they've caught it, too.

Your Fourth Month—Your baby is still fairly small, but oddly enough, you can't fit into even your loosest skirt. So you finally announce your pregnancy and feel guilty because your boss, the cleaning crew and a younger woman who has been eyeing your job all seem happier about the news than you do.

Your Fifth Month—You feel guilty when a coworker overhears you talking on the phone about Zorro—the name you and your husband have given your fetus—and you tell her you're discussing your new pet hamster which, incidentally, is about the size your baby is now.

Your Sixth Month—Your baby now weighs about two pounds, considerably less than your pocketbook. You feel guilty for accepting a seat on the bus from a man, thus setting the women's movement back two decades for fifteen minutes of comfort.

Your Seventh Month—Your baby is now about the size of a small doll. You, unfortunately, are the size of a Beluga whale. You feel guilty for shrieking at the well-meaning cashier in the office cafeteria when she pats your bulging belly and makes you spill the four glasses of milk you swore you would drink.

Your Eighth Month—Your baby now approximates the size of an official NBA basketball and is impossible to cover with a standard-size napkin. You feel guilty for dripping salad dressing down the front of one of the two maternity dresses that now constitute your entire wardrobe.

Your Ninth Month—Your baby is now the size of a child who wears 0–3 months clothing. You feel guilty for spending an entire week at work studying layette catalogs and then receiving a memo from your boss saying you're great for continuing to work so hard. You feel guilty because you've begun glaring at coworkers who, panicked by the idea that they'll have to deliver your baby themselves, greet you each morning with the words, "Still here?"

An awful lot of guilt here, huh?

And this is just the beginning.

AN EXCERPT FROM "ASK MISS ETIQUETTE"

Dear Miss Etiquette:

I've just discovered I'm pregnant, and I'm worried that my "condition" will hurt my professional image. What can I do to make sure my coworkers will still take me seriously?

Karen
Milwaukee

Dear Gentle Reader:

Congratulations! Miss Etiquette loves babies and is always pleased to hear someone else is expecting one. And she most certainly appreciates your desire for a proper pregnancy. She has heard horrendous tales of expectant mothers who talk publicly about such intimate matters as disrupted digestive systems, swollen ankles and other afflicted body parts too private even to name. Then they wonder why their colleagues think they've lost their minds rather than gained a small companion.

As the first step in your admirable quest to do the Correct Thing, you should attempt to keep your pregnancy secret for as long as conceivably possible. (Under most circumstances, Miss Etiquette has the utmost disdain for puns, but she finds that one irresistible.) Miss Etiquette remembers hearing how her dear mother disguised her own condition for six months with a wardrobe of conservatively striped lawn tents. If loutish colleagues inquire about your changing silhouette, you may turn on your heel and walk away. More explicit expressions of anger are unacceptable, particularly in a mother-to-be.

When concealment is no longer possible, you should make a formal announcement of what we shall delicately call your confinement. This should be done in as decorous and businesslike a manner as possible. A staff meeting, an interoffice memo or a revised business card are appropriate ways to let colleagues know you are in a family way.

This announcement should be the first and last time your condition is ever discussed. Miss Etiquette knows that will be difficult because people often feel that a pregnant belly is public property. But it is incumbent on you, as Lady in Waiting, to discourage that notion. If your stomach is so obtrusive that all conversation stops when you walk into a room, you might consider entering backwards. At meetings, you might cover your belly with a clipboard or notebook.

Office chitchat must also be avoided. If you run into a coworker in the office cafeteria and she asks you what you're having, look her straight in the eye and say, "Tuna on white."

Generic Food Corporation

KAREN DEVANEY
Group Manager

BABY ON BOARD

POSTPARTUM GUILT

Immediately after giving birth, you may feel guilty that . . .

- You stopped working an entire week before having your baby, while your best friend, a mergers and acquisitions lawyer, closed a multimillion-dollar deal with a Japanese company when she was FULLY EFFACED and having contractions TEN SECONDS apart.
- You worked up until the day you delivered and ended up having a caesarean, which never would have happened if you'd taken a month off to rest like your mother-in-law suggested.
- You didn't bond the instant the nurse handed you your baby. Instead, your first thought was that you still looked six months pregnant, and you wondered if you'd ever be able to fit into your clothes again.
- An hour later, you still hadn't bonded. Instead, you worked the phone. You called your parents, your college roommate, your next-door neighbor, your hairdresser and the well-meaning cashier in the office cafeteria. Then you called your boss to remind him you want your job back and he'd better not try to replace you while you're on leave.
- A day later, you had bonded so completely you couldn't even remember what your job was. When your coworkers visited you in the hospital, you insisted on showing them the first diaper you'd changed.

WHAT COMES NEXT . . .

maternity leave (syn. parental leave, family and medical leave, vacation time plus accumulated sick days)—**1.** A period of unspecified duration but generally too short. **2.** A time when a formerly energetic working woman can't get out of her nightgown until midafternoon. **3.** A period of weeks, months or years when a husband comes home from work and says, "So what did you do today, honey?" and his wife honestly answers, "I have no idea."

WHAT YOU EXPECT TO GET DONE WHILE ON MATERNITY LEAVE

Teach the baby to say "Mama"
Stencil the walls in the baby's room
Visit your college buddy and her three kids
Refinish the antique potty chair you found at a flea market
Make a videotape of the baby for forty-five close friends and relatives
Stock your freezer with pumped breast milk
Fill in first entries in *My Baby's First Year* book
Implement *14 Days to a Tighter Tummy* exercise plan
Update your résumé
Screen and interview at least three dozen potential baby-sitters
Take "beauty rests" while the baby is sleeping
Clean out your basement
Go to first-run matinees with the baby in a Snugli
Stitch the baby's name in needlepoint

WHAT YOU ACTUALLY DO

4.78 tons of laundry

PART TWO

The Guilt Inducers

**Some of the
Three Zillion Things
That Make Us Feel Guilty**

CHAPTER 2

Our Kids

"**T**hey grow up so fast."

You've been hearing that comment almost from the morning you brought your tiny, moist bundle home from the hospital. And for the most part, you've shrugged it off.

But now it's the last day of your maternity leave, and you're out pushing the stroller in the park when a grandmotherly type stops to admire your adorable six-month-old. "Enjoy your baby," says the sweet old lady as she walks away. "Before you know it, he'll be in college."

Suddenly, an alarm goes off in your head: *What am I doing? These are precious moments, he's changing every day, and I'm about to miss it all. Why in the world am I going back to work?*

You look down at your baby, who is growing so quickly he's gained four pounds in the past two minutes. In another half-hour, he'll be asking you for the car keys.

Your Guilt Attack continues: *This poor thing needs his mother. That baby-sitter seems nice enough, but who knows? She'll probably keep him in a playpen all day. Maybe he'll forget who I am. He'll grow up feeling unloved . . .*

By now, your adorable six-month-old is looking more and more like a pint-size drug addict, toting an Uzi, heading off to Alcatraz, screaming at you, "IT'S ALL BECAUSE YOU WORKED, MA!" (Look, the baby-sitter's name is tattooed on his left arm!)

Fortunately, your child's gurgle breaks the spell. Whew, he's six months old again! Before long, you're able to be rational: *I've had six months to bond with my baby, and it's been great . . . but I'd kind of like to talk to grown-ups again . . . and, without my salary, we can barely pay the mortgage, let alone save for college.*

You're feeling pretty secure again and your son is looking more and more like his happy little self. (That tattoo was just strained peas.) Still, a bit later, when you see that meddling old woman heading your way, you beat a hasty retreat—just in case she hits you with another zinger that lands you back on that roller coaster of Working Mother Guilt.

GUILT isn't restricted to Working Mothers, of course. Like exhaustion and exasperation, it's something all moms share. But when you're a Working Mother, you tend to forget about the universality of maternal guilt. Buried deep in your psyche, somewhere between your Social Security number and the recipe for Play-Doh, is the belief that if you were home full-time with your children, you'd be the Perfect Mother. Calm. Patient. Creative. And—who knows?—if you're a dumpy brunette, maybe even a willowy blonde.

And somewhere in your kids' psyche—next to the part that figured out that asking for water at bedtime can buy fifteen more minutes—is an instinct for triggering your guilt at any age. So your two-year-old, hearing the microwave beep, chirps, "Dinner's ready." Or your three-year-old, in an all-too-familiar tone, lisps to his stuffed teddy bear, "Hurry up." Or your five-year-old calls her new lunchbox a briefcase. Or your ten-year-old complains that he couldn't get started on his homework until 8 P.M. because you weren't there to make him do it.

Usually you deal with it with aplomb. Usually you're too tired to do anything else. But every once in a while, you get a full-fledged Guilt Attack like that panic in the park. And when it strikes, it COMPLETELY AND TOTALLY distorts reality.

Maybe it happens when the day-care center calls to say your toddler doesn't feel well. Without even asking for details, you leap from your chair and race to the emergency room on the theory that the woman didn't want to tell you over the telephone HOW NEAR TO DEATH HE REALLY IS. You spend hours navigating the hospital bureaucracy before giving up and driving to the day-care center. There you find your little boy in circle time, singing "Baby Beluga in the deep blue sea . . ."

"He seems much better now," the day-care worker says, as you throw up.

Or maybe, on the way to work, you pass a bookstore and notice a publication, *365 Creative Things to Do with Your Children on Rainy Days*. You suddenly have visions of yourself home with your kids, blissfully shaping an old bleach container into a piggy bank. Minutes after you buy the book, you remember that your children are twelve and sixteen and, if you ever attempted such a project, they'd look at you as if you'd just lost your mind and say, "This is really dumb, Mom."

AFTER your Guilt Attack has subsided, you're inclined to agree with them. Whew! You're rational again, and there's one thing you know: You're a pretty good mother. Maybe even a very good mother. A Perfect Mother? Okay, so maybe not. Your standards and expectations are awfully high, and you suspect that no matter what you did, perfection would remain elusive.

And there's something else you know too: You haven't got time for guilt. What free time you've got is better spent enjoying these precious moments with your child. After all, like the old lady in the park said, pretty soon he'll be in college . . .

Oh look, over there! Isn't that him now? Climbing out of his stroller, sharpening his No. 2 pencils and heading out to take his GREs . . .

DETERMINE YOUR MOTHERING STYLE or
What Kind of Mother Are You, Anyway?

YOU KNOW YOU'RE A FAST-TRACK MOM IF:
- You are a lawyer, a banker, a senior manager, or another professional required to wear gabardine suits in subdued colors.
- You've ordered at least $500 worth of equipment from The Right Start catalog, including at least one of the following: an educational black-and-white mobile for your newborn; an overpriced stroller made in the same country as your foreign car; a light-bulb–operated contraption that warms diaper wipes.
- Your favorite book is *Raising a Gifted and Talented Child*.
- You feel guilty that you didn't hire a "developmental consultant" to work with your nanny like one of the partners in your firm did. Or, if you did, you feel guilty that she wasn't effective enough to get five-year-old Emily Rose into the kindergarten that feeds directly into Harvard.

YOU KNOW YOU'RE A TOUCHY-FEELY MOM IF:
- You work as a psychologist, social worker or substance abuse counselor, or in any other of the "helping" professions.
- You belong to a Working Mothers' Support Group.
- Your favorite book is *Raising Your Child's Self-Esteem*.
- You feel guilty because the last time two-year-old Sigmund had a "Time Out," you neglected to follow up with a meaningful discussion about what he was feeling when he bit his playmate, grabbed his truck and shouted, "MINE!"

YOU KNOW YOU'RE AN ARTSY MOM IF:

- You are in a creative field and make your living, albeit barely, as an actress, artist, photographer or writer.
- You wear either gauze skirts and Birkenstock sandals, or only outfits that are black, including stockings, sunglasses and flat-heeled shoes.
- You order your children's clothing from a West Coast outfit called After the Stork, and your daughter owns at least three hats.
- You feel guilty that you never find time to sit down with Chloe to do any of the activities described in your favorite book, *1001 Creative Projects for Your Child and You.*

YOU KNOW YOU'RE A SUBURBAN MOM IF:

- You work in a traditionally female field, such as teaching, nursing, or doing anything at all preceded by "para."
- You live in a house that looks identical to your neighbors' and you order your clothing from J. Crew, Lands' End or L. L. Bean.
- You'd like to buy your kids clothing from the same catalogs, but they insist on labels like Esprit, Ocean Pacific and Nike Air Jordans, which you can only get at the mall.
- You feel guilty because Katie isn't keeping up with the Joneses' kid, who is a champion in swimming, soccer, T-ball, Little League, lacrosse and karate. And because you don't have a bumper sticker on your four-door minivan, like they do, that says, "My child is an honor roll student at Tractville Elementary."

YOU KNOW YOU'RE A CATCH-AS-CATCH-CAN MOM IF:

- You work, but are hard-pressed to remember your job title or official responsibilities.
- You once wore an inside-out blouse to the office.
- You can't find the time to buy your children clothing, and if it weren't for your nephew's hand-me-downs, your son would be wearing his sister's pink pajamas to school.
- You feel guilty about practically everything, often with very good reason.

A PROFILE OF A "CATCH-AS-CATCH-CAN" MOTHER

NAME: Karen Devaney

HOMETOWN: Milwaukee, Wisconsin

AGE: Thirtysomething

ACCOMPLISHMENTS: Keeping her job while raising her two small children, Josh, 5, and Nora, 2—with a little help from her husband, Robert (Bob) Fried, of course.

LAST BOOK READ: *What to Expect When You're Expecting*

HOBBIES: "Are you kidding?"

QUOTE: "Whatever I'm Doing, It Isn't Enough."

DRINK: Anything but apple juice.

ASK THE EXPERT . . .

Below is a conversation between a worried Working Mother and a child development expert with a beard, a soothing voice and a bunch of letters after his name. The regular type indicates what the psychologist actually says. The italics indicate what the guilt-ridden Working Mother *hears* him saying:

Q: *My maternity leave lasts only three months (substitute six weeks, six months, two years, fourteen years, whichever applies). Will it be harmful to my child if I go back to work at this time?*

A: There is no "perfect" time to separate from a small child. Developmentally, each stage of infancy and toddlerhood exhibits distinct tendencies toward what we call "separation anxiety." However, the separation can be managed in a way to minimize stress on both parties.

Yes, three months (substitute six weeks, six months, two years, fourteen years, whichever applies) is the very worst time to go back to work.

Q: *From a psychological standpoint, what is the best kind of child care for my baby?*

A: Children can cope well within a variety of settings provided that minimum standards are met. In searching for a caregiver, a parent should look for someone who is warm, caring, affectionate and attentive.

They're all horrible. Babies need their mothers.

Q. *Although she used to sleep through the night, my one-year-old now wakes up repeatedly. Is this related to the fact that I'm working?*

A. Such sleep disturbances are common. It is around this age that the child begins to realize that she is separate from her parent, and that gives rise to feelings of anxiety, which often manifest themselves at night. While you can try to reassure her, this is a fundamental stage of child development.

Absolutely, she doesn't see enough of you during the day.

Q. *My child suffers from recurrent ear infections. Is that because I'm working?*

A. That's out of my area of expertise. I'd suggest you ask your pediatrician.

I don't want to be the one to tell you, but the answer is probably yes.

A CONVERSATION WITH THE DEVIL'S ADVOCATE
About Missing Those Important "Firsts"

DEVIL'S ADVOCATE: Don't you worry that you're going to miss out on some of your child's important developmental milestones? His first word, his first step, his first tooth . . .

WORKING MOTHER: (Sigh!) Of course I worry. I feel awful. I feel terrible. Some days I feel like killing myself. (Sob!)

DEVIL'S ADVOCATE: Oh stop now, you're being ridiculous. Nothing in childhood happens suddenly. It's all a gradual process. C'mon, do you really think a kid's tooth pops just like that? Do you really think, in a single moment, he goes from complete silence to one articulate first word?

WORKING MOTHER: You're right! I feel better already . . .

DEVIL'S ADVOCATE: You should worry about the really important things, like that you won't be around the first time your child runs into a concrete wall, cracks open his lip and has to be rushed to the emergency room for stitches . . .

WORKING MOTHER: (Gasp!) I worry about that too . . .

DEVIL'S ADVOCATE: Aaahhh, don't worry. You'll be around for that. In fact, it will probably be your fault . . .

WHAT'S YOUR Q.T.I.Q.

Quality Time: It's something every Working Mother strives to spend with her children. But at best it's elusive. Here's a true/false quiz to help you determine whether you know what Quality Time really is.

1. **QUALITY TIME** is like an orgasm; you know it when you're having it.   **TRUE**   **FALSE**

2. To be having **QUALITY TIME**, you and your child need to be in the same room.   **TRUE**   **FALSE**

3. The term is used correctly in this sentence: "Come on, sweetie, I've got two minutes. Let's hurry up and have a little **QUALITY TIME**."   **TRUE**   **FALSE**

4. It does not count as **QUALITY TIME** if either you or your child is asleep.   **TRUE**   **FALSE**

5. The best opportunities for genuine **QUALITY TIME** occur on family vacations.   **TRUE**   **FALSE**

6. Psychologists agree that **QUALITY TIME** can compensate for a lack of quantity of time parents spend with their children.   **TRUE**   **FALSE**

1. This is definitely **FALSE**. In most cases, **QUALITY TIME** occurs spontaneously, often without your even knowing it. For instance, you may think you're having a family picnic when, in fact, you're actually having **QUALITY TIME.**

2. This is **FALSE**. You can be having **QUALITY TIME** if your son is in his room playing with Legos, and you are downstairs in the kitchen baking brownies, provided, of course, that the smell of chocolate is wafting upstairs and he is thinking, "Boy, do I have a great mom!"

3. This is **FALSE**. As we said before, true **QUALITY TIME** occurs spontaneously and, typically, without your knowledge. Most deliberate attempts to have **QUALITY TIME** are unsuccessful, particularly if they are in time chunks of five minutes or less.

4. This is definitely **TRUE**. However, on those particularly hectic days when you feel especially guilty about not spending enough time with your kids, you may wish to convince yourself otherwise.

5. This is definitely **TRUE**, as long as you **DO NOT** vacation at Walt Disney World during Spring Break.

6. This is definitely **FALSE**. Psychologists **NEVER** agree about anything.

MURPHY'S LAWS FOR GUILTY WORKING MOTHERS

1. Your child will inevitably be sick on one of the two days of the year when it's **ABSOLUTELY IMPERATIVE** for you to be at the office.

2. After you leave your child at the day-care center, she will scream and cry for exactly the same amount of time it takes for you to walk out of hearing range.

3. Your child's school will declare a snow day only if the at-home mom who's offered to cover for you in emergencies is stranded out of town.

4. Your school-age children will call you at work to mediate a dispute within three minutes after your Female Boss with No Kids comes into your office to discuss Important Business.

5. On those mornings when you need to leave the house early, your five-year-old will throw a major temper tantrum because you ran out of Cheerios.

6. In a lunch-hour race to your daughter's school to catch the class play, you will end up stuck in traffic caused by the only eighteen-car pileup in the freeway's history.

7. The president of your company, making his semiannual rounds on your floor, will pop his head into your office at the exact moment you begin putting updated photographs of your children into the stand-up frames on your desk.

8. Your son's championship soccer game will be scheduled to coincide with your industry's once-a-year out-of-town convention.

9. Your children will rip up, crayon or spill things on Important Papers **ONLY** if it is mandatory that they be delivered to a client first thing in the morning.

10. Your caregiver will inevitably be sick on the other of the two days of the year it's **ABSOLUTELY IMPERATIVE** for you to be at the office.

THE GREAT DEBATE: GUILT AND FAMILY SIZE

With the birth of your first child, you are likely to get a heaping dose of Working Mother Guilt. But what happens to your guilt level when subsequent children arrive on the scene?

Like any significant question, this one elicits great debate. To present both sides of the issue fairly, we asked two articulate and opinionated Working Mothers to comment on the following statement: "You experience less guilt with your subsequent children than you do with your first."

Here's what they said:

Working Mother #1: This is absolutely true. With your first child, you take parenting extremely seriously. You read books titled *Raising Baby Right* and *What to Expect Every Minute of Your Child's Entire Existence*.

You focus on every detail of your child's life, right down to the color of his nasal discharge. You monitor each stage of development with excitement and anticipation. You exclaim things like, "Oh look, Bob, Josh is about to roll over!"

As a result of this near-obsession, you are more acutely aware of WHAT YOU ARE NOT DOING and WHAT YOU'RE DOING WRONG.

Consequently, you are overwhelmed by guilt all the time.

However, with your second, third, fourth or, Heaven forbid, fifth child, you do not have any time to read books, and your interest in nasal discharge has seriously waned.

You miss some developmental milestones completely, and wouldn't mind missing a few others. You exclaim things like, "Dammit, Bob, Nora's going to roll down the stairs!"

Because you are so carefree with subsequent children, you have no expectations and ideals and, consequently, no standards to violate. Therefore, you experience significantly less guilt than you did with your first.

Working Mother #2: This is absolutely untrue. You feel far guiltier with subsequent children, because now you are stretched beyond your limit. All the balls you had been precariously juggling have tumbled far and wide. And so you feel guiltier than ever about your failure to keep them all in the air.

You feel more guilt because you are not devoting the same amount of attention to subsequent children that you did to the first. (Note the "did." You no longer "do," and you feel guilty about that as well.)

For example, you photographed and videotaped your first child on average every 1.6 days. You even have a picture of the first time he pooped in the potty. By contrast, you have only two photos of your second child: the day she came home from the hospital, which your neighbor took with his new Canon Sure Shot, and her ninth birthday.

You've noticed, however, that your subsequent children are much more independent and capable than your firstborn. But rather than alleviate your guilt, this realization exacerbates it. It reminds you of the saying, "Raising kids is like making pancakes. You never get it right with the first one."

And so you feel even guiltier knowing that you've probably screwed up child number one.

GUILT REDUCTION EXERCISE #1

*D*o you feel completely overwhelmed by guilt? Maybe you're exaggerating your condition. Chances are good that you're not really as guilt-ridden as you think. Let's try a simple exercise to prove this point.

Listed below are typical statements made by Working Mothers. Probably in the flush of new motherhood, you've made them all yourself. Put a check next to each vow that—now that you've been a mother for a while—you've broken, without a twinge of guilt or even the bat of an eyelash.

———— "I will never let my children watch television."

———— "I will never let my children watch commercial television."

———— "I will never let my children watch more than two hours of commercial television in one sitting."

———— "I will feed my children only healthy, nutritious snacks."

———— "I will never send my child to school with a cold."

———— "I will never bribe my child to do anything."

"I will never lose my temper."

"I will never be inconsistent in my disciplinary methods."

———— "I will never say, 'Because I'm your mother, that's why.' "

———— "I will never say, 'You dirty little sleazeball, I'm going to box you upside the head.' "

SCORING—For each check, give yourself ten points. If your score is:

0 TO 10—If your child is more than six months old, you probably harbor a lot more guilt than is truly necessary. Lower your standards a little. You'll feel better.

20 TO 50—You're still too idealistic. You probably aren't spending enough time with your kids.

60 TO 90—You're doing great. By the time your children are in high school, you'll be practically guilt-free.

100—Congratulations. You have absolutely no standards at all. Seek professional help.

CHAPTER 3
Our Careers

Whose crazy idea was it to schedule a meeting for 4:45 P.M. anyway??!!!?

That's what you're thinking at 5:32 P.M. as you sit in a conference room, listening to your boss's newest business plan: to sell mainframes to the Amazons.

While he raves about this remote, unexploited market, your mind is ten miles away (twenty-one minutes without traffic) at the day-care center. That's where your child is waiting for you with an overworked and underpaid aide who, even now, is vengefully calculating your $75-per-minute late charge.

You tune back into the office discussion just long enough to hear an enthusiastic colleague—the same politically correct young woman who lobbied for a "smoke-free environment"—suggest that 1 percent of profits from this venture should go to save the rain forests. As she launches into an elaborate cost-benefit analysis, you do a little analysis of your own.

Already your late charge at the day-care center has topped the three-figure mark. And your kid and the day-care aide are probably sticking pins in a doll they've named after you.

You mutter something about an urgent appointment and make a graceless exit.

"I'm outta here."

NOT all that long ago, you were a rising star, a fast-track individual who was the first one in each morning and the last one out each night. You were promoted so often that even you secretly wondered if it had anything to do with the company's affirmative action policy.

Now you fear you might be on something called the Mommy Track, which seems a lot like being derailed.

You've never asked for any special consideration, but it's clear your priorities have changed. Last month when you were invited to a posh retreat to reevaluate your company's long-term strategy, you politely declined because you wanted to stay home to reevaluate the contents of your kids' toybox.

And now that you've skipped out on this important meeting, you worry that you've irreparably damaged your career. After all, this isn't the first disappearing act you've pulled. Last month, when your son appeared as a woodpecker in a school play, you missed the training session on the new Executone phone system. Now every time you try to transfer a call, you hook the caller into your own voice mail.

Your trouble balancing work and family hasn't escaped your colleagues' notice. At lunch the other day, the new research associate told you that, after watching you for a week, she's decided not to have a family. Terrific, you thought, as you gulped down your yogurt. Once you thought you'd be a role model for younger women. Instead you're a walking advertisement for Norplant.

Still, so far your boss has been oblivious to any problems. At your last performance review, he gave you such high marks that you stuck one of your son's gold stars on your forehead. And there's fight in you yet. So the night after the meeting where you went AWOL, you think about ways to get back on track.

The next morning, you invite your boss to lunch. You vow not to bring up the F-word (Family) even once. This isn't easy. When you open your car door to let him in, you realize your daughter's carseat is still up front. An easygoing guy, he says he doesn't mind sitting in the back. He even whistles along with the Raffi tape that starts up the second you turn on the ignition.

At the restaurant, though, things go pretty smoothly. You fight your temptation to cut his meat. You talk business. You point out that conditions in the Amazon are fairly primitive, starting with a lack of electricity. You suggest that laptop computers might be more appropriate. You use words like "optimize" and "comparative advantage." He seems impressed.

He is impressed! The next week, he calls you into his office to announce you've been promoted again. You're going to be in charge of the entire export operation. Your personal assistant will be that enthusiastic young colleague, Ms. Earth Day herself.

As usual, you feel conflicted. You're already having a rough time of it, and the promotion will mean more work. You'll have to find excuses not to visit the Amazon. But you decide to concentrate on the benefits of Getting to Yes. You'll have a little more flexibility; maybe you'll even be able to do some work at home. You'll finally be earning enough to pay for child care. And, as a boss, you'll be able to make important executive decisions. Like when to schedule meetings.

Never again at 4:45.

THE WORKING MOTHER'S MONTHLY BUDGET

INCOME

GROSS INCOME		$3,000
Less federal, state and local taxes	($1,200)	
Less FICA	($ 300)	
Less contribution to United Way	($ 50)	
NET INCOME		$1,450

EXPENSES

Payment on second car	$200
Commuting costs: gas, tolls, parking, etc.	$ 75
Nora's day-care	$400
Josh's after-school care	$250
Cleaning lady (twice a month)	$ 80
Clothing budget	$ 50
Pantyhose	$ 50
Drycleaning and stain removal	$ 50
Coffee, doughnut for breakfast at desk	$ 25
Salad, diet soda for lunch at desk	$ 65
Take-out Chinese food for dinner at home	$ 40
Take-out fast food for dinner at home	$ 80
Deliver-in pizza for dinner at home	$ 40
Necessary medications: Maalox, Excedrin, Tums	$ 20
MONTHLY EXPENSES	$1,425

ACTUAL BENEFIT OF WORKING

$25/month

or $5.81/week
or $1.16/day

29

ALTERNATIVE SCHEDULES
FOR WORKING MOTHERS

A full-time job would drive many mothers absolutely and irreversibly bonkers. So instead, they opt for Alternative Work Arrangements or Alternative Work Schedules, commonly known as AWAs or AWSs. (Ever wonder what your infant meant when he was making those AWA-AWA-AWA-AWA sounds? Now you know.) Here's a quick summary of the various options:

Part-Time—An arrangement where you squeeze forty hours of work into three or four horribly hectic days and are thereby freed up to take care of grocery shopping, laundry, car-pooling, doctors' visits, housecleaning and lawn maintenance on your "day off," which is generally the same day your immediate supervisor schedules Very Important Meetings.

Flex Time—An arrangement where you go to work at four in the morning and, if you're lucky, get to go home at three in the afternoon, at which time your coworkers, just getting down to the day's business, look at you as if you're a lazy flake.

Job Sharing—An arrangement whereby two equally harried Working Mothers try to approximate one level-headed, responsible employee and, in the process, naively give some Capitalist Pig Boss two heads for less than the price of one.

Seasonal or Temporary Work—An arrangement in which you forgo job security, advancement, professional stature—not to mention health insurance and a regular paycheck—in exchange for the opportunity to work your butt off for four months and scramble beyond belief for acceptable child care.

Work at Home—An arrangement where no one believes you are doing anything, especially your boss, who calls only when your two-year-old is in the midst of a temper tantrum or when you've run out to buy Infant Tylenol.

Sequencing—An arrangement where you take fifteen leisurely years off to raise your family happily and then easily slide back into a prestigious and high-paying career. Unfortunately, there is only one truly desirable "sequencing" slot in the universe and that has been filled by Supreme Court Justice Sandra Day O'Connor.

FROM THE IN/OUT BOX OF KAREN DEVANEY

August 14
T O : Staff
F R O M : B.A. Mann
　　　　Office of the Chairman

I'm delighted to announce that, effective Sept. 4, Steven Fasttrack will be vice president of marketing for Generic Foods Corp. As you all know, Steve has had a meteoric rise since he was hired by Junk Food group manager Karen Devaney in 1986 as an assistant brand manager for Crunchie Munchies. It was Crunchie Munchies' phenomenal success that led to GFC's stock split in 1987. For the past two years, Steve has been running the Tokyo and London offices simultaneously.

In his new capacity, Steve will oversee the Junk Food group, as well as advertising and public relations.

August 15
T O : Steve
F R O M : Karen

Steve, great news about your promotion! It'll be wonderful working with you again—and I'm sure Susan and the kids will be thrilled to have you at home.

Let's get together at the first opportunity to discuss strategic planning for Junk Food. I'm afraid I'll be out of the office for the next two weeks (my baby-sitter is going on vacation), but hope to meet with you as soon as I return.

August 16
T O : Karen
F R O M : Steve

Thanks for your note. Great to have you on my team. Shall we start with breakfast Sept. 5 at 7:30 A.M.? In the meantime, can you ship me your five-year strategic plan?

August 17
T O : Steve Fasttrack
F R O M: Karen

Sorry, I just can't make it in that early. Could we schedule it for early afternoon? (I have to leave by 5.) I'm enclosing the plan, which is virtually complete. Pages 5–14 got stuck together—I'll try to get you a fresh copy before we meet. Sorry!

September 4
T O : Staff
F R O M : Steven Fasttrack

I'm delighted to announce that, effective Sept. 5, Kimberly Singleton will be manager of the Junk Food group for Generic Foods Corp. As you all know, Kimberly has had a meteoric rise since she joined GFC's advertising department in 1988. Her campaign on the nutritional value of Crunchie Munchies was one of the main reasons for the brand's resurgence last year.

Karen Devaney will become an assistant manager for public relations, which I'm sure will be thrilled to have the benefit of her years of experience at GFC.

DOS AND DON'TS FOR AVOIDING THE MOMMY TRACK

You, too, can avoid the Mommy Track to nowhere by following these simple rules:

- DON'T ever let on that your children are an important part of your life. While at work, make comments like, "I'm not going to let some twenty-five pound blob of howling toddler get in the way of my career." Although no one will know quite how to react, this will give them the impression that you don't have a maternal bone in your body, and may even win you a promotion.

- DO make it appear as if you're engaged in Terribly Important Business when dealing with family matters on the job. When phoning to arrange for a clown to perform at your child's fifth-birthday party, talk in muted, serious tones and take voluminous notes, preferably on a yellow legal pad.

- DON'T keep pictures of your children in your office. If you've got any there, replace them with framed copies of *Sports Illustrated* covers or, better yet, hunting trophies. The bigger the game, the better. If it's an endangered species, better still.

- DO give your colleagues the impression that you are a workaholic who's on the job nonstop. If you have to get up in the middle of the night to deal with a youngster's nightmare, seize the time to leave messages on coworkers' voice mail. Use a suitcase instead of a briefcase to carry work home. If you're truly bent on making this point, buy two identical cars and leave one permanently in the company parking lot so colleagues will think you're always at work.

- DON'T ever let on that you have to leave the office to see a school play, do car-pool duty or pick up a sick child. Have an excuse handy if someone catches you on your way out the door. Some effective nonmotherly alibis: "I have to meet my broker to talk about mortgage-backed securities." "My mechanic needs a hand overhauling my car's engine." "I'm meeting a buddy for a quick game of racquetball."

- DO dress for success, i.e., as much like a man as possible. Wear every symbol of authority your frame can bear: Dark suits with padded shoulders, boring but sensible shoes, cufflinks and, if at all useful in your line of work, a holster and gun. Always remember to check your "power" clothing for spitup stains and small fingerprints.

BEST/WORST JOBS FOR WORKING MOTHERS

Working Mothers do everything from digging ditches to directing multimillion-dollar business ventures. But some careers are better suited than others to the Working Mother life-style. Here's a look at some of the best and worst jobs:

BEST JOBS

WORST JOBS

Nursery-School Teacher
A mornings-only job ideally suited to mothers of the pre-school set. Typically, nursery schools permit employees to bring along their own children, thus allowing you to spend genuine quality time with your kid while collecting a paycheck.

President of the United States
A well-respected, high-profile position that allows you, as Chief Executive, to call your own shots. Perks include travel to exotic places, photo opportunities with important people, weekends in Camp David and good-looking Secret Service agents available to baby-sit around the clock.

Nursery-School Teacher
A low-status, low-wage job that means, when you're not taking care of your own kids, you're taking care of someone else's. But because typically nursery schools permit employees to bring along their own children, you're usually taking care of your own kids too. Enough is enough.

First Lady of the United States
The original Mommy Track slot. A demanding, round-the-clock job in which you work terribly hard for no pay, have your appearance continually critiqued in the press and are viewed mainly as your husband's sidekick. Another downside: After four to eight years, you have to look for another job.

BEST JOBS

Morning News Show Anchor

A high-paying and glamorous job that affords women a miraculous ability to give birth after only two months of visible pregnancy, then return to work three weeks later, as svelte and vivacious as ever. An added perk: You and your offspring will definitely be asked to model for the cover of a mass-circulation magazine.

Time-Management Consultant

No explanation needed.

Air Traffic Controller

A responsible and challenging position with regular hours, good health benefits and decent pay—even without a union. The work is so absorbing that the day literally flies by. Another plus: Colleagues are likely to be polite males who trained in the military and will call you ma'am, not mom.

WORST JOBS

Evening News Anchor

It's unclear why this lucrative and glamorous career is not a good one for Working Mothers. However, that is undoubtedly the case because, in the entire history of television, not one mother has worked in this capacity, except as a weekend substitute, which conflicts with the children's days off.

Beauty Consultant

No explanation needed.

Air Traffic Controller

A demanding and stressful position in which you are responsible for thousands of lives daily. This job has all the drawbacks of being a mother (multiplied thousands of times) but none of the rewards.

GUILT REDUCTION EXERCISE #2

Let's try a little exercise in positive thinking.

Instead of casting the chores of motherhood in a negative light, why not gild the lily a bit and see them as skills that might sound impressive on our résumés.

Be creative. Use your imagination. See how easy it can be:

WHAT YOU'RE DOING	RÉSUMÉ DESCRIPTION
Convincing Josh to stop pulling Nora's hair	**Negotiation**
Getting two kids out of diapers	**Training**
Figuring out how to save for college while paying for child care	**Budget Analysis**
Buying no more baby gear and toys than you have space for	**Inventory Control**
Getting Josh to put his dirty clothes in the hamper	**Delegating**
Making a French horn out of a paper-towel roll	**Product Development**

CHAPTER 4

Our Husbands

Someone is nuzzling your breast.

It's 2 A.M., hours since you collapsed in bed in your flannel bathrobe. Now there's a familiar sensation around your nipple. Wait a minute?! You weaned your baby months ago. Or did you? You're too groggy to remember. Through a haze of sleep, you instinctively reach out to cuddle your—omigosh!—husband!

It's hard to say which was the first casualty of childbirth—your waistline or your relationship with the man you married. But clearly both have suffered. Not so long ago, he was your friend, your lover, your confidant. Today he is primarily "your dad," as in "Go ask . . ."

Sex was the first thing to go. Your child's conception wasn't immaculate, but almost every moment since then has been. First you were afraid you'd lose the baby. ("I don't want to be paranoid, but . . .") Then you were too sick. ("I really do have a headache.") Then you were too huge. ("Are you kidding? I need a crane just to turn over.") Then you were too sore. ("Not tonight, sweetheart, I feel like the doctor left his forceps inside me.")

And ever since children arrived on the scene, thoughts of romance have pretty much departed from your mind. Given the choice of sex or sleep these days, sleep wins. Hands down.

On balance, it's probably just as well. Even if you had the energy for sex, it's unlikely you'd have the privacy. With the kind of luck you've been having lately, your toddler would wander into the bedroom looking for his teddy bear just as you were . . . oh, never mind. Suffice it to say he'd be traumatized for life, and it would have nothing to do with a lost teddy bear.

Besides, who can think about sex with a man you haven't had a one-on-one conversation with in months? Come to think of it, you barely even see the guy anymore. In the name of Getting Something Done, you take the baby while he fixes the screen door; he takes the baby while you make dinner; when he gets to the breakfast table, you race for the shower; when you get home from work, he heads upstairs to give the kids a bath.

You two are apart so often that even your children have begun wondering if there's only one of you, a gifted transvestite. The last time you were all in the same room—last weekend? the weekend before that?—the baby began to cry.

IF you are a typical guilt-ridden Working Mother, you probably blame yourself for the demise of your relationship. After all, you should know better. You've read the Ann Landers columns about middle-aged men who take up with buxom twenty-year-olds because they don't get what they need at home. You've seen the articles in women's magazines telling you that a Relationship needs to be Nurtured.

As a mother of small children, you feel like you're already doing all the nurturing one woman can possibly handle. But never one to pass up a challenge, you feel compelled to rekindle the flame. (Forget the romance. You're mainly motivated by the nightmarish prospect that your relationship will fall apart and you'll be left alone with the kids.)

You dig out an article on relationship nurturing and try to follow the advice of The Experts. "Make a date with your husband," the pros suggest. So you do. Dinner for two at a quiet restaurant. Linen-covered tables. Candlelight. Soft music. The whole ball of wax.

The big night comes. Fortunately, so does the baby-sitter. Out on the town, you feel a bit out of place. It seems like this is the first time in a hundred years you've been at a restaurant where you don't get a balloon and a packet of crayons with your menu. But you have a drink, and after a while, you start to relax. Luckily, there's plenty to talk about. What the baby spat up today. How many letters your preschooler knows.

It doesn't take long before you feel pretty comfortable. There's something to be said for going out without kids. You don't have to tip heavily to make up for the Cheerios all over the carpet. You can leave the table without looking back to make sure you collected the contents of the diaper bag.

By the end of the evening, you're even feeling somewhat—could it be?—romantic. You remember why you married your husband. You've started calling him by his own name. Outside, you walk under the stars hand in hand. In the car, you move the baby seat and drive home side by side. You get into the house, pay the baby-sitter, check on the children, and you're ready for, ahem, bed.

Or almost ready.

First, you've got to find your diaphragm. There it is, hidden behind the soap paints and the bottles of Ipecac. The contraceptive jelly is harder to come by. You hunt for a half-hour before remembering that you hid it so you'd stop confusing it with the Desitin.

Finally, feeling almost sensual, you head to the bedroom. You crawl beneath the sheets and reach over to your husband. But wait. Something is wrong with this picture: He's sound asleep. You can't wake him.

In truth, you're not all that disappointed. The thing that really bothers you is knowing that he won't even feel guilty in the morning. And knowing that if it were you who'd fallen asleep instead, you'd agonize about it for days.

From The Working Mother's Must Read File:

AN EXCERPT FROM *COSMOPOLITAN* MAGAZINE

HOW TO GET GOOD—NO, GREAT— SEX BACK IN YOUR LIFE!

It's been 184 days since the last time you and your husband had sex, but who's counting? Well, you are! Sure, you're tired, but you suspect you'd warm up once things got hot and heavy. The question is, how can you light that old fire?

Karen, a Milwaukee, Wisconsin, marketing executive with two children, says that what works for her is slipping into a negligee, dimming the lights and pretending that her husband is really Kevin Costner. She insists that it isn't Kevin's achingly attractive buns, but his reputation as a devoted family man, that turns her on.

"Sexual fantasies should have some basis in reality," observes Dr. Marie Kaplan, a psychiatrist at the Mind-Body Institute in New York. "For working mothers, an appropriate sexual fantasy would probably involve an idealization of some aspect of her life. It might be as simple as fantasizing that the laundry's been done."

Susan, a high school teacher in Los Angeles and mother of two, likes to pretend she looks just like another California career woman with two kids—Jane Fonda. "I imagine I have this great bod," she says, adding, "I try not to think about Ted Turner."

Mind over matter. You do it every day. Well, you can do it every night, too.

Of course, even if you've got the will, the kids tend to get in the way. Here are some simple techniques you can try:

• Turn on the TV. For X-rated sex, sit the kids in front of a G-rated video. Chip 'n' Dale will give you time for a quickie and a shower. And for the kind of marathon sex you used to have, offerings range from *The Little Mermaid* to *Charlotte's Web*. Press "Play" and as soon as the credits roll, head for the bedroom. Pretty soon, you'll start thinking "SEX" the minute you see "DISNEY"!

• Sneak out of the office early. You already spend 90 percent of your work day on personal matters. Make it 95 percent. Lynn, a psychoanalyst in Portland, Maine, slips away every week or two for a rendezvous with her husband at a friend's apartment. She maintains that her patients don't even notice she's gone.

• Try a new location. The changing table is a bit small, but have you thought about the sandbox? Or the swing set, after dark? "Given how desperate she is, the working mother will welcome almost any change," says Dr. Kaplan.

Now that you know your options—get going!

HOW NOT TO HAVE SEX

No luck in putting the pizzazz back in your love life? Or—be honest!—no interest? Whatever the case, here's a tested and proven strategy for avoiding sex.

As soon as your husband starts making overtures, return his caresses, run your fingers through his hair and whisper in his ear:

"Isn't it time to think about having another baby?"

COMMUNICATING WITH YOUR MATE

Before Children, you and your husband were soulmates. You could talk for hours about your hopes and dreams, about politics, religion, the arts, the Meaning of Life.

Now that your life's replete with meaning, however, there doesn't seem to be much room for conversation. Not that you don't have plenty to discuss: where to send your daughter to preschool, how much allowance to give your son, how badly your best friends' kids behave. The problem is finding the time.

Don't despair. You can still have a conversation with the Man in Your Life. To help, we offer some popular channels of communication for Working Moms and Dads:

Post-It Notes on the fridge: These force the writer to get to the point quickly (Do the laundry! Feed the hamster!) and are hard to overlook. Limited space, however, makes them a less-than-ideal vehicle for discussing the Meaning of Life or even the value of Pre-K.

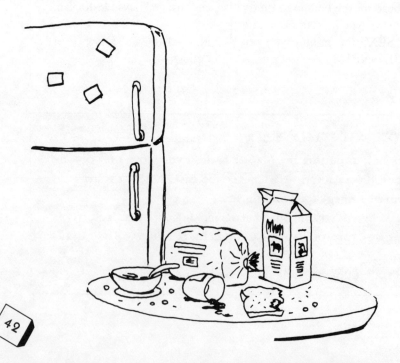

Voice Mail/Fax—These have all the advantages of high-tech: They're immediate, impossible to ignore and unambiguous. But the message should be as businesslike as the medium. Given their public nature, they would be inappropriate, for example, for a discusson of your husband's pathological attitude toward money.

In the car—This is usually a favorite venue for animated discussions about directions, but there's no reason that it couldn't be used for a heart-to-heart about, say, his mother. Unless, of course, the kids are in the back seat and awake.

Through the kids—You might try using children as a way of conveying information. They're accessible, quick and cheap. The problem is that they tend to be as unreliable as that old party game, Telephone. If, for example, you ask your eight-year-old to tell his dad that you need the checkbook, the message is likely to come through as: "Mom says I can play another game of Nintendo before I start my homework."

Greeting Cards—Hallmark makes cards for every occasion, and with a little imagination, you can use them to send your mate any number of messages. A retirement card ("Not working anymore?") will hint that you don't think he's doing enough around the house; while a sympathy card ("Sorry about your loss!") can let him know you're sensitive to the fact that he's balding.

CHAPTER 5
Our Bodies, Ourselves

i t's Saturday morning at the shopping mall.

You've come to buy shoes for your little girl.

Suddenly, you are overcome with memories of how you once loved to shop. You have an idea: Why not turn this errand into a pleasant little shopping spree, the kind you used to enjoy with your girlfriends? You'll browse through the racks for a while, then maybe stop for a light lunch . . .

CRASH!

Oh no! Your shopping companion—age three—has just yanked down a mannequin and sent her plastic head rolling into the cosmetics department.

Oh no! That real-life mannequin at the Clinique counter is coming toward you. She's so enraged that you worry she's about to knock the head off your precious child.

Like fugitive shoplifters, you race for the nearest exit. From the safety of your car, you catch your breath and review the situation. Probably it was all for the best. Even if you had stayed at the mall, you wouldn't have been able to treat yourself to anything. (Funny what a family does to "disposable income," isn't it?) And even if you could afford new things, you're better off without them. Your baby would pull out those new hoop earrings in no time, leaving your earlobe—and possibly your baby—permanently scarred. You'd wear that new silk blouse all of three times before it came back from the dry cleaner's with one of those familiar little tags, "Sorry, we were unable to remove this stain."

ONCE upon a time, there was enough time and money to take care of Our Bodies, Ourselves. To go shopping. To get manicures. To read the newest books, see the newest movies, discuss the newest news. To play tennis, ski, jog to the health club to stay in shape.

These days, staying in shape seems as challenging as a tennis match against Martina Navratilova. For a while, you had some legitimate excuses. When you were breast-feeding, you needed the milk-producing capability from the cellulite on your thighs. And until the baby slept through the night, you were so sleep-deprived that the only exercise you could handle was Rapid Eye Movement.

Now, though, you have No Excuses—like the brand name of the jeans you can't fit into. But you still can't find ten minutes to race over to your health club to renew your membership, let alone time to do aerobics with flat-stomached teenagers in neon tights!

Dieting hasn't worked too well either. You're great at skipping lunch, but your weaknesses are leftover quarters of peanut-butter sandwiches and handfuls of Goldfish crackers, which must certainly contain an addictive ingredient.

You could half tolerate your neglected body if your mind wasn't deteriorating along with it. It wasn't all that long ago that you were a witty and intelligent woman. You were INFORMED. Now, you only use the newspaper to make silly boats, and if the television is on at all, it's tuned in to *Wake, Rattle and Roll*. You're become so remarkably out of it that when you heard a colleague mention Fergie and Di, you thought it was a new Saturday-morning cartoon.

You wish you weren't neglecting yourself, but, quite frankly, on your list of "Things to Take Care Of," your name is way down there at the bottom—along with your pet hamster Zorro.

So you try to keep a positive attitude. The only thing worse than being an out-of-shape, unhealthy bimbo is being a miserable, out-of-shape, unhealthy bimbo. And, after all, things could certainly be worse. You still can name the president and vice president of the United States. You haven't yet gone to work in your bathrobe. You continue to hold down a demanding job, so your mind must be in some kind of operating order.

And certainly you don't regret the trade-offs you've made. At least for now, your children are devoted, loyal and thoroughly admiring little fans.

The other day when you came home from work feeling as disheveled as a street person, your four-year-old son looked at you and said, "Mommy, you're beautiful."

So what if he's at the height of his Oedipal phase?

It made you feel just terrific.

BEFORE   AFTER   TEN MINUTES LATER

A WORKING MOTHER'S WISH LIST

- A weekend at the spa
- A live-in pediatrician
- Meals on Wheels
- Legislation outlawing snow days
- Scotchgard for blouses
- A male boss with a working wife
- A week at the spa
- A wife (non-working)
- A female boss with children
- Two years' severance
- Two weeks at the spa

A QUIZ: HAS YOUR MIND TURNED TO MUSH?

Maybe you were a board-certified genius. Or maybe you could at least balance your checkbook. It really doesn't matter. There's something about having a child or two that turns the best brain to mush. Your memory goes first; your mind quickly follows. Overnight, you've forgotten the periodic table of elements, the dollar-yen exchange rate and what time the dry cleaner's closes. All you can remember is, "Daddy's taking us to the zoo tomorrow, zoo tomorrow . . ."

To measure how many neurons you've got left, we offer this Working's Mother's IQ test. There are no points for right answers because, as they say in early-childhood development, there are no right or wrong answers. Besides, you'd probably have trouble adding up a score.

For each name, choose the most appropriate definition:

Plato
a) Greek philosopher
b) Modeling clay

Michelangelo
a) Great Renaissance painter
b) Hero on a halfshell

Calvin
a) French theologian
b) Small boy with stuffed tiger named Hobbes

Barbie
a) Infamous Nazi war criminal
b) D-cup doll

Charlotte
a) The largest city in North Carolina
b) A spider

MOST COMMON ILLNESSES IN WORKING MOTHERS

Not so long ago, you were healthy and fit. Today, you pick up every germ your children bring home from school. They get sick and recover in a matter of hours. You get the same ailment and feel wiped out for a month.

But in addition to the usual colds and flus, Working Mothers are also prone to the following illnesses. Don't be surprised to discover you already have some of them.

Chronic Fatigue Syndrome—A low-grade illness that results in a feeling of constant tiredness. Medical researchers are still puzzling over what causes this mysterious disease. Working Mothers, for their part, are puzzling over why supposedly intelligent medical researchers can't figure it out.

Chronic Stress Syndrome—An illness whose symptoms include a sense of being frazzled, overwhelmed and at loose ends. Acute attacks are common in the morning as you're racing to get out of the house and again in the early evening when your children are tired, hungry and cranky and so are you. Among cures being developed are the establishment of an "extended day program for mothers," i.e., twenty-eight hours instead of twenty-four.

NJF Disease—A long-term illness characterized by droopy breasts, a flabby abdomen and, usually but not always, thick thighs. Fortunately, most patients can lead a normal life with the help of an appropriate wardrobe. This disease is so named because those who are afflicted are forced to acknowledge they are NJF—Not Jane Fonda.

Total Burnout—A disease with a sudden onset. After months of functioning at a manageable, albeit frenzied, pace, a sufferer of this ailment suddenly decides she CAN'T TAKE IT ANYMORE and runs off to Tahiti —*sans* children—with a swarthy millionaire named Raoul. Unfortunately, this disease is rare and not contagious.

GUILT REDUCTION EXERCISE #3

Do you avert your eyes when you pass a mirror? Flinch when you open your closet? Panic on Election Day because you don't recognize a single name on the ballot? And do you still feel guilty because you're not the woman you once were? Here's an exercise that will soon have you patting yourself on your rumpled back.

In the first column, make a list of those things you did in your childless years. (Don't stop to marvel at how, back then, you were crazy enough to think you were busy and stressed out.) In the second column, list those things you do now, in the same amount of time. We've jotted down a few of our own just to get you started. Compare lists and congratulate yourself on how much more efficiently you're using your time.

THEN	NOW
Shower and dress	Get children out of bed
	Ask children to get dressed
	Beg children to get dressed
	Dress children yourself
	Skip shower
	Dress yourself (if there's time)
Read paper and sip coffee	Gulp half-cup of coffee
	Referee battle over prize at bottom of cereal box
	Hunt for lunchboxes
	Throw out yesterday's sandwich
	Scrape curdled milk from Thermos
	Make PB & J sandwiches (again)
	Reheat coffee in microwave
Spend lunch hour at gym	Drive to son's school for car-pool duty
	Persuade five kids to get in car
	Fasten four seat belts around five kids
	Listen to scatological rhyme
	Drop off rowdy children at assorted locations, usually on one-way streets
	Drive back to office

_____   _____

_____   _____

_____   _____

_____   _____

_____   _____

CHAPTER 6

The Home Front

One evening as you drive home from work, you have a marvelous fantasy, and it has nothing to do with sex.

You imagine that your house has been immaculately cleaned by an obvious professional, not a corner-cutter like you. When you close your eyes, you can see fresh-cut tiger lilies on your polished oak table. What's that smell? Oh, yes. Pine-scented ammonia on your sparkling window-panes. And that sound? The breeze whistling through the empty laundry basket. Ahh, you think, so this is heaven. . . .

But when you arrive home, open the door and step on the same clump of lime-green Play-Doh you sidestepped this morning, reality hits. Oh well, even if the house were clean, it would never stay that way for long. Better wipe up the Play-Doh before someone steps on it again.

■ ■ ■

FORGET the frills. Being a parent entails providing your child with the basics—food, shelter and clothing—under minimum federal standards. But some days, the minimum seems awfully high. Things have gotten so out of hand that you're tempted to hire a road maintenance crew to plow out your house. The only thing stopping you is the fear that they'll file a complaint with the Board of Health.

No one would dare suggest you're not trying. It seems you're forever wiping apple juice off the living-room sofa and scraping caked-on Rice Krispies off the kitchen floor. One day last week, you used the Dustbuster so energetically that you practically vacuumed the diaper right off the baby. But if housekeeping is war, you may as well surrender.

Your kids don't mind the mess, of course, but you do. Before Children, you became accustomed to a modicum of domestic order. Remember when you could find things? When you could walk through a room without stumbling over a single primary-colored piece of plastic? When you even believed—is this possible?—that there really was such a thing as the joy of cooking?

These days, preparing dinner seems more insurmountable than the Himalayas. On a good night, you can manage frozen fishsticks and macaroni and cheese. On a bad night, you convince yourself that potato chips are a vegetable. Your idea of a terrific meal? Easy! One that's delivered to the door in thirty minutes. (Good news: If it isn't, you get it for free!)

On the bright side, dinner's out of the way in a matter of minutes. And, in a couple of hours, so are the kids. Then, finally, lucky you: You get to clean up the mess in the kitchen!

Sure, your husband helps out with the household chores. Some of your most intimate moments lately have been while you sweep and he loads the dishwasher before you both collapse into bed. But you can't help noticing what a high tolerance the American male has for chaos and clutter.

Take your husband—please. He has an uncanny ability to sit in a chair piled high with dirty clothes and read the newspaper. You, on the other hand, pick up the clothes, put them in the washer, transfer the load that's there into the dryer, and fold the dry load. By the time you get around to the newspaper, all you want to do is throw it out so it doesn't stay on the floor all week. Your husband suggests you're compulsive. You tell him he's a slob.

One would think by now you'd have developed the ability to look beyond a sloppy house and view it simply as a price of modern life. You know that housekeeping standards everywhere have taken a precipitous decline. In your head, you understand that's because women work outside the home, and, thank heavens, have better things to do with their time than scour soap scum off bathroom tile. But in your heart lurks the nagging feeling that when the mirror in your bedroom doesn't sparkle, it's a foggy reflection on you.

Where this notion comes from is a great mystery. Maybe it's because you want to do everything your mother did—in addition to everything your father did. Maybe you feel guilty that you're not providing the Perfect Home for your husband and kids. Or maybe just beneath your feminist veneer lurks a traditional housewife in a calico apron.

Who knows?

Figuring that out could take years, and really, your time is better spent mopping the kitchen floor.

Dear Reader:

▶ Are you tried of reading magazines that seem written more for Julia Child than for someone who finds convenience foods too much of a hassle?

▶ Are you sick of looking at photographs of family rooms that seem to belong to June Cleaver when the one in your home looks more like Chuck E. Cheese after a busy Saturday?

▶ Are you fed up with suggestions that you fill your child's lunchbox with carrot sticks shaped like bunny ears and cheese sandwiches cut out like small teddy bears?

If you've answered yes to any of the above questions, we'd like to welcome you to the premiere issue of our new and exciting publication:

BATTERED HOMES AND GARDENS

This is a magazine that understands the busy routine of today's working mom. A publication that knows that, try as you might, your home will still look like the highway to Kuwait after Saddam Hussein rolled in.

In upcoming issues, read these informative articles:

▶ A how-to piece on "Hands-Off Gardening."

▶ A groundbreaking medical report on why kids can actually thrive on Peanut Butter and Jelly 365 days a year!

▶ 101 Gourmet meals you can prepare with no tools other than a can opener!

▶ A step-by-step guide to making your own window treatments in only 15 seconds!

▶ An interview with a psychologist who discusses why women in the post-feminist age actually give a damn about their homemaking skills. (With special tips box on getting over this hang-up.)

In the meantime, we're sure you'll love these articles in this issue. And remember, as they say on the streets, a battered home is better than no home at all!

Sincerely,

The Editors

MEALS IN MINUTES (REALLY!)

Yes, we know you're skeptical. You've attempted recipes called "Meals in Minutes" before. And every time, they've ended up taking you a full half-hour, plus at least that time to persuade your child to eat what you've made.

But now *Battered Homes and Gardens* offers you Meals in Seconds.

For those really hectic evenings, we offer these serving suggestions that, barring any unforeseen disaster, you truly can prepare, serve, and sometimes even get your kids to finish in minutes. Two or three minutes, that is. Not thirty.

A Banana—Someone's mother once said that a banana contains the right balance of vitamins and minerals to sustain a child. It is unclear over what period of time this is true. Or if it is true for all age groups. Or, in fact, if it is true at all. (Someone's mother is dead, and we cannot pursue this further. Nor can we find anyone else who will make the same assertion. However, we like this notion and are willing to give it the benefit of the doubt.)

There are any number of ways you can get your child to eat a banana. You can slice it onto a plate and tell your child he's having "banana coins." Or you can cut it horizontally and call it "banana fingers." Or —if you're feeling really lazy—you can hand your child a whole banana and tell him to eat it like a monkey.

Then you can place the small round Chiquita sticker on your child's forehead as a reminder that you've gotten him to eat a banana and he's had a sufficient balance of vitamins and minerals to sustain him.

Any way you slice it, mealtime will be apeeling.

A Bread Sandwich—Kids love bread, and there's nothing more convenient—or varied—than a sandwich. Give them whole wheat between two slices of white. White on rye. A triple-decker, whole wheat on white on rye. Or if you want to get fruit into their diet, try raisin bread on whole wheat. One extra advantage of this meal is that it travels well and requires little cleanup.

Beans on Toast—All the fiber your child could ever need. This is a little more involved but, if you're fast with a can opener, you can whip this up in ninety seconds. If your child balks, remind him that thousands of people in Britain, Australia and New Zealand eat this every day. Also point out that they eat spaghetti on toast, too, and at least you're not giving him that.

Anything Delivered to the Door with the Exception of the Newspaper—You usually can convince your children to eat anything that's delivered to your home. This is especially true if it comes in a large flat box and is carried by a man who drives a beat-up Ford Pinto with a cardboard sign precariously positioned on top.

CLUES FROM CLAUDIA

Dear Claudia:

With two young children and a full-time job, my house is always a mess. I've learned to live with the chaos, but the stains on the carpeting really get to me. Do you have a hint on an easy way to keep them clean?

Beverly in Buffalo

Why not pull up the carpeting and put down asphalt? It's inexpensive, never shows the dirt, and your kids will be able to roller-skate anywhere!

Claudia

Dear Claudia:

I never used to get around to dusting and mopping, but now my baby does it for me. As he crawls around the house, he collects all the stray debris. At the end of the day, I just throw him in the bath. Then I scour the tub—and the house is immaculate.

J. McD
Portland, ME

Sounds good, as long as his tetanus shots are up to date.

Claudia

Dear Claudia:

I'm totally sick of doing laundry. Any tips on how to cut down on the number of loads I do each week?

Karen in Milwaukee

A simple solution: Leave Milwaukee and move to Florida, where kids can run around in a bathing suit all day.

Claudia

ODE TO THE MICROWAVE

Microwave, my microwave.
Countless minutes you help save.
It's only beeps from ice to plate,
A Working Mother's second mate.

Baby's Bottle: forty-eight
Last night's rice: One minute eight
Grandma's Oatmeal: ninety-two
Program "cook" if it's hard to do.

Full power run makes fish sticks tough
But cuts the time; that's good enough.
For whine control, it's the only way.
Kids scream: "When's dinner?" "Now," you say.

If you had to choose, which would it be,
Your husband or beloved G.E.?
Men can help in many ways,
But it's tough to compete with microrays.

So tote that timber, chop that wood,
The good old days weren't all that good.
Stoke the stove, you kitchen slave.
I'd rather have a microwave.

A CLIP FROM *USA Today*

Dinner Hour Is Family Hour for USA

When it's chow time, the family still chows down together, according to a survey by *USA Today*. Of 1,000 households polled, 95 percent said they eat "as a family" on most nights. Here's how those households described a typical "family meal":

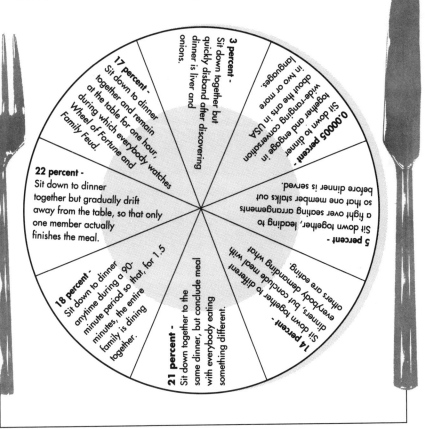

3 percent - Sit down together but quickly disband after discovering dinner is liver and onions.

17 percent - Sit down to dinner together and remain at the table for one hour, during which everybody watches Wheel of Fortune and Family Feud.

0.0005 percent - Sit down to dinner together and engage in wide-ranging conversation about the arts in USA in two or more languages.

22 percent - Sit down to dinner together but gradually drift away from the table, so that only one member actually finishes the meal.

5 percent - Sit down together, leading to a fight over seating arrangements so that one member stalks out before dinner is served.

18 percent - Sit down to dinner anytime during a 90-minute period so that, for 1.5 minutes, the entire family is dining together.

14 percent - Sit down together to different dinners, but conclude meal with everybody demanding what others are eating.

21 percent - Sit down together to the same dinner, but conclude meal with everybody eating something different.

PART THREE

The Guilt Provokers

Some of the Characters in Our Lives Who Make Us Feel Guilty

CHAPTER 7

The Stay-At-Home Mom

Maybe she's a twenty-five-year-old New Traditionalist who cans her own peaches, bakes her own pies, sews her own clothes.

Or perhaps she's a thirty-nine-year-old former corporate executive who graduated with honors from the London School of Economics.

She could be anyone. Your next-door neighbor, a onetime colleague, your own sister, a good friend.

But in your mind, she is mainly one thing: a Stay-At-Home Mom. And, boy, can she drive you nuts.

WHO knows why you let her get under your skin?

Maybe you're the competitive type who sees her doing everything you think you should do, and then some.

When it's your day to bring the school snack, you rush out for a bag of Cheese Curls and a few cans of Hawaiian Punch. When it's her turn, she shows up with homemade granola bars and fresh-squeezed carrot juice. You console yourself knowing that the kids, at least, prefer your snacks. But deep in your guilt-ridden soul, you worry that she's a BETTER MOTHER THAN YOU.

Already there are signs that her kids are coming out ahead. The night before the school science fair, you helped your son put together a project to illustrate a fundamental but important scientific concept: Water boils at 212 degrees. The Stay-At-Home Mom and her daughter spent an entire month building a machine that could analyze the molecular structure of acid rain.

Guess who won?

When you ran into the Stay-At-Home Mom at the playground, she was in the sandbox counting pebbles with her toddler, while her six-year-old waited his turn for the swing. You, meanwhile, were shrieking at your two-year-old to get off the top of the monkey bars, while your five-year-old shouted, "Jump!" You didn't feel any better when the woman gave you a sympathetic smile. She's so perfect, you thought, she ought to be canonized: Our Lady of the Park.

OR maybe the Stay-At-Home Mother bugs you because she makes you commit the cardinal sin of Envy. You'd never let her know it, but there are days you'd be happy to trade your life-style, such as it is, for hers. She shops. She naps. She exercises. In the morning, as you race to your car with your toddler in tow, she's out pushing the stroller to the park. "Great day, isn't it?" she calls out. She might as well say, "Isn't it a pity you'll be stuck in a windowless office while I spend the day outside with my child?" Instinctively, you stick out your tongue.

All right, maybe that's a little immature, but you've got your reasons. After all, the Stay-At-Home Mom is *supposed* to be your enemy. Remember *Newsweek*'s cover story about the Mommy Wars? It was right up there with the conflict in the Persian Gulf and the carnage in Cambodia. Hey, you're a good soldier. If war's been declared, you're ready to fight.

OR maybe it's that you simply don't understand the Stay-At-Home Mom. You can't figure out why, in the 1990s, an intelligent woman would be willing to forgo the rewards that come with a responsible job and a respectable salary. Doesn't she ever feel envious of her husband's career? Doesn't she get bored being home with her kids? Doesn't she sometimes feel like an anachronism? Who does she think she is, anyway—Donna Reed?

You'd love to ask her, but you're afraid she'd hit you with her diaper bag. Or, more precisely, you're terrified to hear what she'd have to say. If she is politic, she'd probably tell you that she believes women should be respected for doing whatever they choose. If she is forthright, she might say that she's chosen to stay home because she firmly believes small children are best raised by their mothers. If she's a zealot, she might even tell you what she really thinks: that children of working mothers will grow up without self-esteem or the capacity to form lasting relationships or the ability to count pebbles.

But if she is honest and open and self-confident—not to mention a good enough friend—she might confide that she's not completely comfortable with her role. She might tell you she feels lonely at the playground when the only other grown-ups around are maintenance men and bums. She might say she worries that she's a poor role model for her daughter. She may even admit she feels guilty because she's not Doing It All.

Guilty? Did someone say guilty?

You like the way that sounds. You don't want to gloat at her discomfort, but maybe the Stay-At-Home Mom wouldn't irk you so much if you knew she felt a little guilt. At least then you'd have something in common.

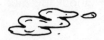

THE MOMMY WARS: GIVING PEACE A CHANCE

Are you ready to do your part in ending the Mommy Wars? It's time for a truce. In the spirit of reconciliation, we offer guidelines for soldiers in both camps. Follow these rules, and maybe it will lead to a long-term cease-fire. Maybe then to rapprochement. And eventually—who knows?—to a New Domestic Order.

FOR THE WORKING MOTHER:
HOW TO GET ALONG WITH THE STAY-AT-HOME MOM

1. Don't ever say anything that indicates you think her mind has turned to Jell-O just because she spends her entire day going around in a circle saying "Ashes, ashes, all fall doooowwwn . . ." Talk to her only about weighty and complicated subjects, even if it's hard to get her attention because she's going around in circles. Suggested topics: Bank Bailouts, Genetic Engineering, Antifeminist Backlash.

2. Don't ever imply that you think SHE IS COMPLETELY AND TOTALLY FINANCIALLY DEPENDENT ON A MAN. Resist the temptation to ask her, for example, if she needs her husband's permission to buy pantyhose—no matter how curious you are. Remember that she probably doesn't need pantyhose anyway.

3. In fact, don't ever suggest that the main reason she can stay home is that she had the good sense and foresight to marry a MAN SHE *CAN* COMPLETELY AND TOTALLY FINANCIALLY DEPEND ON. Don't say, for instance, "Gawd, I wish I'd married an investment banker instead of a classics professor so I could sit around the playground all day." She might get the impression you are jealous.

4. Don't invite her to cocktail parties. If you do, she will inevitably run into someone who, by sheer coincidence, will get stomach cramps and race to the bathroom the second she mentions she is home with her kids. The Stay-At-Home Mom will then tell everyone

she knows that people at YOUR cocktail party walked away from her because she doesn't have a career.

5. Don't ever ask her to do anything for you, even if it would be totally effortless for her and a major hassle for you. You can break this rule in extreme circumstances but, when you do, say something compassionate and understanding, like, "I realize you're planning a very hectic day at the sandbox, but would you mind terribly if I asked the UPS man to leave the replacement part for my mother's pacemaker at your house?"

FOR THE STAY-AT-HOME MOM:
HOW TO GET ALONG WITH THE WORKING MOM

1. Remain calm when she talks to you as if your mind has turned to Jell-O. Resist the temptation to say, "Who the hell do you think you are anyway?!?!?!? I have an M.B.A. from Harvard, and all you have is a liberal arts degree from some third-rate land-grant college." Instead, humor her. Ask her if she'd like to play Ring-Around-the-Rosie.

2. Don't flinch when she implies that your relationship with your husband is "traditional" while hers with her husband is "liberated." Don't mention that the goal of the women's movement was to give women choices, not to have them dress in dumb suits and dopey little bow ties. Also don't tell her that you don't see anything liberated about her racing off to work every day and then coming home exhausted to cook and clean while her husband plays racquetball.

3. Don't try to talk sense to her when she tells you she's working because she can't afford not to. Don't point out that, after she pays for child care and commuting, she's probably operating in the red. Refrain from adding up how much money she'd save just on pantyhose if she were at home.

4. Don't invite her to join your playgroup. This will remind her that she doesn't have enough job security to take a couple of hours off work during the week to hang out with her child. Or if she does come, she will inevitably run into the only Stay-At-Home Mom in your group who would rather debate the relative merits of Pampers vs. Luvs than discuss, say, antifeminist backlash—thus confirming her suspicions that Stay-At-Home Moms have minds of Jell-O.

5. Don't hit her over the head with your diaper bag when she asks you, for the zillionth time in a month, to drive her whiny children to school since she has an "important appointment" and "you're going there anyway." She's so run-down that the slightest injury could result in hospitalization, in which case you will undoubtedly end up chauffeuring her children for her entire convalescence.

HOW TO DISGUISE YOURSELF AS THE PERFECT STAY-AT-HOME MOM

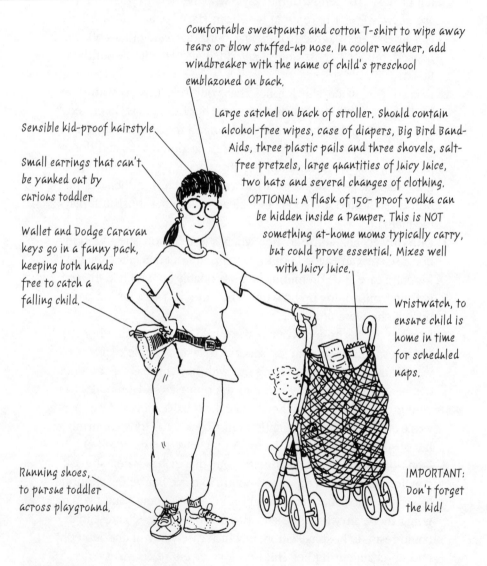

Comfortable sweatpants and cotton T-shirt to wipe away tears or blow stuffed-up nose. In cooler weather, add windbreaker with the name of child's preschool emblazoned on back.

Sensible kid-proof hairstyle.

Small earrings that can't be yanked out by curious toddler

Wallet and Dodge Caravan keys go in a fanny pack, keeping both hands free to catch a falling child.

Large satchel on back of stroller. Should contain alcohol-free wipes, case of diapers, Big Bird Band-Aids, three plastic pails and three shovels, salt-free pretzels, large quantities of Juicy Juice, two hats and several changes of clothing. OPTIONAL: A flask of 150-proof vodka can be hidden inside a Pamper. This is NOT something at-home moms typically carry, but could prove essential. Mixes well with Juicy Juice.

Wristwatch, to ensure child is home in time for scheduled naps.

Running shoes, to pursue toddler across playground.

IMPORTANT: Don't forget the kid!

68

CHAPTER 8

Our Own Mothers

Remember the good old days?

The plate hit the table at six o'clock, minutes after Dad walked in the door. The house was always spotless. No waxy yellow buildup on those kitchen floors. You never had to burrow in the laundry basket for a clean blouse. And if you got sent home from school sick, there was always someone waiting.

Dear old Mom!

Maybe she wasn't the *perfect* mother when you were growing up. Maybe the fruit did always sink to the bottom of her Jell-O molds. But her few flaws have faded with the passage of time. And now that you've got a family of your own, all you can recall from childhood is what a terrific mom you had.

Funny, that's all she can remember, too.

Her superior mothering skills are the only thing you two can agree on anymore. These days, she's forever finding fault with what you do and how you do it. She doesn't understand why you put in so many hours at your job. Why you can barely get a comb through your daughter's hair, when she got you to stand still for a perfect part and braids. Why your son is allowed to wear torn jeans. (She patched them before you could explain that you paid an extra $10 for the rips.) Why dinner's at eight, or maybe nine, or on bad nights, maybe not at all.

When you first announced you were pregnant, you expected your mother to be thrilled. (After all, isn't imitation the sincerest form of flattery?) Instead, dear old Mom wondered aloud how you would manage it all. And now that it's clear you're not managing, you half expect her to report you to the child welfare people.

Wait a minute!

Maybe you're rewriting history a little. Maybe the moms of yesteryear weren't so wonderful after all. Cast your mind back—way back—to those days. Consider the norms of the fifties and sixties:

- **Prenatal Child Abuse.** What did Mom give up for you when she was pregnant? Coffee? Cigarettes? No way! In fact, she yielded to every craving. She ate so much ice cream along with her pickles that you ended up with a body that's 87 percent fat cells. No wonder you can maintain a perfect weight only on 100 calories a day.
- **Just Say Yes Childbirth.** Now practically illegal! Back then, mothers-to-be could choose between a two-week stay in the hospital, completely medicated, or a home birth with a pot of boiling water. Amazingly, your mom chose drugs. That explains why you're so groggy these days. Come to think of it, that's probably what's wrong with your relationship with Mom. She was so spaced out that you two never had the chance to bond.
- **Breast Wasn't Best.** In all likelihood, you were given a bottle of sugar-laced, sodium-loaded formula the second you came out of

the womb. Cracked nipples? Engorged breasts? Not for Mom! She wasn't about to make those sacrifices for you.

■ Nutrition by Nitrates. An acceptable childhood diet consisted of nitrate-packed bologna, white bread that helped destroy strong bodies twelve ways, and—can you believe it?—canned spaghetti. It was years before you learned that "Franco-American" could refer to international relations.

■ Look, Ma, No Seat Belt! It's remarkable to think you ever survived without the fifty-pound carseat with retractable harness and Bakelite shield that's carried your precious cargo since his ride home from the hospital. As a kid, your place was just over the tailpipe of the wood-paneled station wagon.

■ Small-Fry Socialization. Ever feel lonely in a crowd! Have trouble making small talk? Of course you do. You spent your most formative years cooped up in a playpen, which, by the way, had wood slats that would never meet today's safety standards. You, by enlightened contrast, are raising free-range children.

■ Role Modeling. Mom was a housewife—it says so right on your birth certificate—and raised you to be one, too. You're probably still waiting for it to happen, and the word doesn't even exist anymore. The alternative role model back then was Amelia Earhart, but she didn't have kids. So here you are, all grown up and nowhere to go.

THE list could go on and on. But out of respect for the women who raised us, let's stop here. Suffice it to say that your mother didn't have all the answers.

It's a relief, really, knowing you don't have to feel guilty that you're not your mom. In fact, judging from the list, she has a thing or two to feel guilty about herself. Let her make it up to you. Feel free to leave the kids with her any time.

OUR FOREMOTHERS

CRO-MAGNON MOM

Hunter-gatherer. Children raised by wolves.

EGYPTIAN MOMMY

Worked full-time lugging stones to base of pyramid, while children played in empty tombs.

ROMAN EMPIRE MOM

Catered toga parties, circuses; with better child care, could have averted decline and fall.

MEDIEVAL MOM

Nursed victims of cholera and bubonic plague. Taught kids their numbers by counting angels on head of a pin.

RENAISSANCE MOM

Painted Sistine Chapel and invented astrophysics while raising ten beautiful but very chubby children.

SHAKESPEAREAN MOM

Worked as an actor. To get onto the stage, pretended to be a boy so could pretend to be a woman. Kept kids in the wings.

A "HERSTORY" OF THE WORKING MOM

MAYFLOWER MOM

CONESTOGA MOM

DEPRESSION MOM

ROSIE THE RIVETER MOM

EISENHOWER MOM

MODERN MOM

Came to New World as career move, but Founding Fathers took best jobs.

Settled the West as she looked for better job and decent child care (frontier kept moving).

Sold apples on street corner while dodging falling tycoons.

Stoked the fires at home and in munitions factory while Dad made world safe for Democracy.

A historical anomaly. Stayed home full-time to raise children and make mother-daughter outfits in floral prints.

Hunter-gatherer. Children sometimes act as if raised by wolves.

73

THINGS YOUR MOM WORRIED ABOUT	THINGS YOU WORRY ABOUT
Washing whites and darks in the same load	Race relations
Ring-around-the-collar	Drug rings
Napping	Kidnapping
The heating bill	Global warming
Cavities	AIDS
Grass stains	The greenhouse effect
The nuclear bomb	The nuclear family

C H A P T E R   9

The "Other" Mother

Sometime after midnight, you awaken with a start. Was that your child talking in his sleep? It sounded like he was calling out for Mary Ellen, the woman who watches him while you work. Or was he? The house is completely silent now, and—who knows?—maybe it was just some migratory bird. Or your husband snoring. Or a dream.

But maybe he was calling for Mary Ellen. Well, why not? It's important that she means a lot to him. On the other hand . . . c'mon. Not that you're jealous, but why on earth should your son be crying for some other woman before he's eighteen or thereabouts? After all, you're the mother. Mary Ellen is just the . . .

Just the what?

You've never quite figured out what to call her. "Baby-sitter" won't do, because that's the spotty teenager who shows up at your house on

Saturday night with a book bag, a cordless telephone and the key to your refrigerator. "Housekeeper"? Even if she does come to the house to look after your kid, the word doesn't quite fit. Not the way your house looks. "Nanny"? Pretentious. The up-to-date, politically correct term is "caregiver," but that's about as warm as a wet noodle.

So let's call her what she-who-has-no-name really is: your child's Other Mother. Or there's another term: the most important woman in your life.

AS love-hate relationships go, you and the Other Mother have cornered the market. You love her because she loves your child and your child loves her. You hate her for the same reasons.

She's an outsider who knows everything about your child and, by now, probably a lot about you. You're her employer, but you're also her dependent. By taking good care of your kid, she allows you to go to work with an easy conscience. Yet your relationship with her leaves you continually guilt-ridden.

You feel guilty that she's always got at least one kid on her hip while you dash in and out carrying nothing heavier than a handbag. That she changes an estimated 20.3 diapers per day and wipes a nose every 29.4 minutes while the messiest thing you might do is make a fresh pot of coffee. That you don't pay her as much as she deserves, even though it's the going rate and probably more than you can afford. That, although you've been entrusting your child to her for more than a year, you still do a quick survey of her house twice a day to make sure the electric outlets are plugged and there's a gate at the stairs.

That your child—thank goodness!—loves you more than her.

And frankly, she rubs in the guilt even more because she's such a good Other Mother. She's always reproaching you for your son's latest bruise. When he throws a temper tantrum the minute you walk in the door, she tells you he's been an angel until then. After a day's play, he somehow looks less disheveled than when you dropped him off in the morning. On weekdays, he gets a hot lunch and a nap; on weekends, he's lucky to get cheese and crackers and a half-hour doze in the car between errands.

FORTUNATELY, you're sensible enough to overlook your uneasy feelings about the Other Mother. In fact, sometimes you wonder if you could live without her—and you're terrified that, someday, she'll quit on you.

So you bind her to you with velvet chains. You bring her flowers on Mother's Day (and overlook the fact that she doesn't even give you a card). You encourage your child to include her when he draws the family. If she baby-sits at night so you and your husband can go out to a restaurant, you order a third entree and bring it home for her.

But you're terrified, too, that she won't quit on you, that you'll be the one to leave. The other day, when you mentioned that you were thinking of moving out of the neighborhood, she looked as shocked as if she'd, well, lost her child. You immediately backed off. You said you might move across the street. You said you might stay put until your kid turned eighteen.

You almost said that, if you did move, she could keep the kid. But you have to draw the line somewhere. You're his mother, and she's not. In case you ever start to forget that, just ask yourself: Who's the one who feels guilty?

IS SHE A BETTER MOTHER THAN YOU?
Take This Test and See

Many Working Mothers harbor a secret fear that their caregivers are better at child-rearing than they are. Here's a quick exercise that will—definitively, finally and once and for all—determine whether that's the case.

Put a check in the appropriate box next to each question. If you're undecided or you feel it's a toss-up, you can put a check in more than one box.

	YOU	HER
1. Which one of you is more effective in getting your child to sit still at mealtime and eat what's on his plate?	_____	_____
2. Which one of you spends more weekday hours engaged in playful activities with your child?	_____	_____
3. Which one of you is more consistent about discipline and schedules?	_____	_____
4. Which one of you is more mindful of your child's safety?	_____	_____
5. Which one of you takes your child to the pediatrician more often?	_____	_____
6. Which one of you wakes up in the middle of the night when your child cries out?	_____	_____
7. Which one of you buys your child food and clothing and is saving to pay for his college education?	_____	_____

8. Which one of you went through nine   _____   _____
months of pregnancy and a painful labor
and delivery to bring your child into the
world?

SCORING: For questions 1 through 4, each check is worth one point. For questions 5 through 7, each check earns you 50 points. Question 8 is a bonus question, worth 200 points. The better mother is the one who ends up with the highest number of points. The larger the point spread, the better the mother.

GUILT REDUCTION EXERCISE #4

If you're a typical Working Mother, you undoubtedly worry that you're spending too little time with your child—while the Other Mother is spending too much. Maybe you even think she spends more time with your child than you do.

So let's approach this the way you would your job—methodically. Count the hours over the course of a week. Be sure to subtract for naps and bedtimes. Here's a sample worksheet.

Caregiver's time with baby	Your time with baby
9 hours /day	2 hours /day in morning
− 3 hours /day (naps)	+ 2 hours /day in evening
6 waking hours /day	4 waking hours /day
× 5 days /week	× 5 days /week
30 hours /week	20 hours /week

Not so good, huh? Wait a minute! Those are just the workdays. When you include weekends, you get:

10 waking hours /day
× 2 days (weekend)
20 hours /week
+ 20 hours /week
40 hours /week

What's more, you're probably overlooking some precious moments. What about the time you spend each night coaxing the baby back to sleep? To simplify the math, let's say your husband takes care of one night each week. That leaves you with:

20 minutes /night
× 6 nights
2 hours /week (120 minutes)
+ 40 hours /week
42 hours /week

You're hours ahead—and that's not even counting vacations and holidays. But be careful. One weekend away, and you're neck-and-neck with the Other Mother—especially if she baby-sits for you on Saturday night.

Over the years, of course, the tally changes. You phase out the caregiver. Your kid phases out you. In the meantime, however, you've accumulated thousands of hours.

So relax. Take the evening off.

TYPES OF CHILD CARE

Finding quality child care is critical to a Working Mother's peace of mind. But how can you know what's best? We offer a brief description of your options and list the pros and cons for each:

Day-Care Center—A place with a name like "Wee Care" or "SuperTots" that is staffed by caregivers trained to write down the contents of your child's diaper every time they change it.

Pros: Your child will be toilet-trained early and will learn to pee in cute little kid-size toilets and to wash his hands in similarly scaled sinks.

Cons: This kind of care is typically QUITE EXPENSIVE.

Family Day-Care—A real-life home, usually in your neighborhood, where your child is cared for by someone else's mother who probably has more toys—and definitely more patience—than you.

Pros: Your child will spend his days in a cozy, homelike environment where the toilets are standard size.

Cons: This kind of care is typically QUITE EXPENSIVE, unless you're willing to settle for a home where an elementary-school dropout "watches" twenty-four children in her basement, in which case you can probably get full-time care for $19.99 a week. (Beware, however, if she says she accepts coupons.)

Workplace Day-Care—A day-care center that is located in or near the place you work. Typically, the center has a cutesy name connected to the company it serves. (IBM's, for example, is "ibm"; the one at the CIA is dubbed "Little Spooks.") Workplace day-care centers, however, are so rare that the only time you ever come across them is when you read articles titled, "The Two Best Companies for Working Mothers."

Pros: Your child can be the first one among his peers to learn the fine art of commuting.

Cons: This kind of care is typically QUITE EXPENSIVE, despite what you read in those articles about how those two progressive companies subsidize them.

Shared Care—An arrangement whereby you share the cost of an in-home baby-sitter with another family and take turns, by day, week or month, buying large quantities of milk and getting your house completely trashed by one or two children in addition to your own.

Pros: You will have a sympathetic ear when your baby-sitter calls in sick.

Cons: This type of care is typically QUITE EXPENSIVE, because the only reason the baby-sitter wants to care for more than one family's kids is so she can make twice as much.

In-Home Child Care—An arrangment in which a recent immigrant from a third-world country or a God-fearing twenty-year-old from a small town in Utah comes to your house and, if you're lucky, doesn't sit around watching soap operas all day.

Pros: When you're racing around trying to get out of the house in the morning, you can eliminate "Get Baby Dressed" from your list of things to do.

Cons: This type of care is RIDICULOUSLY EXPENSIVE.

Sick-Children Centers—A special place called something like "Chicken Soup" or "Tykelenol" where you can bring kids who are too sick to go to the regular day-care center or to school.

Pros: You don't have to call in sick just because your kid is sick, even though *you* feel ill leaving him in unfamiliar surroundings when he'd rather be home in his own bed.

Cons: This type of care is ABSURDLY EXPENSIVE, but justifiably so because anyone who's willing to take care of someone else's sick children deserves to be handsomely compensated.

WEE CARE TWO—DAILY REPORT   TODAY IS: Wednesday

CHILD'S NAME: Nora D. Fried   CLASSROOM: Toddlers

GROSS MOTOR SKILLS: Nora jumped up and down scream-ing for twenty minutes after her mother left in the morning and then was too worn out to dance with the rest of us to music of South America, which is the culture of the month.

FINE MOTOR SKILLS: After settling down Nora colored maps of Bolivia and Argentina along with the group.

COGNITION: We are starting to recognize shapes and colors.

LANGUAGE: We talked a little about Paraguay and Uruguay, although Nora didn't seem very interested.

INDEPENDENCE/SOCIAL SKILLS: Nora is making progress in getting along with the other children. Today, she gave Pablo (Paul) a big hug and a kiss after her Time Out for biting him.

AM SNACK: Guayabana slices / Empanadas   Note: Nora didn't eat

LUNCH: Black beans and rice   Note: Nora didn't eat

PM SNACK: Cheetos and Hawaiian Punch   Note: Nora ate nicely

TODDLER'S TOILET

TIME: 9 a.m. _____ B.M. ___✓___ Urine _____ Dry

TIME: noon _____ B.M. ___✓___ Urine _____ Dry

TIME: 3 p.m. _____ B.M. ___✓___ Urine _____ Dry

TIME: 5 p.m. _____ B.M. ___✓___ Urine _____ Dry

TODDLER'S NAP: Nora stayed awake during nap-time singing "La Bamba."

SIGNATURE _____ Mary Ellen

83

DAY-CARE: AN INTERNATIONAL PERSPECTIVE

How does the American child-care system differ from others around the world? Here's a look at what some countries offer working parents:

Sweden—Although all day-care is government-funded, there are more than enough slots for the country's children under the age of five. Teacher-child ratio is 2 to 1, as mandated by government legislation. Regulations also require that all children wear name tags, as even the Swedes can't tell one blue-eyed, towheaded toddler in a primary-color jumpsuit from another. By law, center furniture comes from Ikea and the school bus is made by Volvo. Children learn facts of life at eighteen months, a second language at two years, a third language at three years, and how to pay taxes by five years.

Russia—Because all day-care is government-funded, there aren't nearly enough slots to go around. Officially, there is a ten-year wait to get into one of the centers, but access is faster through the black market. The result is that children in day-care tend to be quite mature, and sometimes go straight from kindergarten into the labor force, bypassing years of schooling. Centers are run by elderly babushkas, with a ratio of one babushka per ten children. Food is awful, and there isn't enough of it. However, the expectation is that, as conditions change, things will get worse.

China—All day-care is government-funded, and space is limited to one child per family; there is no official policy on gender, but enrollment tends to be 99 percent male. Fantasy play, including dress-up, is strongly discouraged. Children learn to share, play in groups of 500 or more, and flood the rest of the world with zillions of cheap electronic goods and plastic bath toys.

France—Centres Du Jour are all government-funded and staffed by stylish but uppity women who teach children ways to snub anyone who doesn't speak French. Children eat particularly well: croissants for breakfast, meats with rich sauces for lunch, and foul-smelling cheese for afternoon snack. Despite this rich diet, toddlers learn to maintain a slim physique.

United States—Virtually no day-care is government-funded. In fact, the government has consistently refused even to acknowledge that day-care exists, despite endless political rhetoric about "family values." Because there are no national standards, day-care centers vary enormously in availability (one for the entire state of Montana), price ($12,000 per child annually in New York, $19.99 in Louisiana) and teacher-to-child ratios (1 to 3 in Wyoming, 1 to 23 in New York). The only factor that remains consistent nationwide is that day-care center workers earn less than dogcatchers, garbagemen, bicycle messengers and twelve-year-old newspaper carriers.

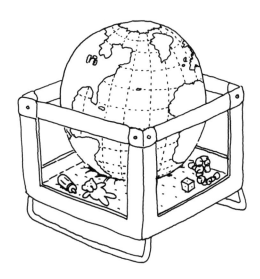

CHAPTER 10
The Supermom

look, up in the sky!

It's a corporate lawyer.

It's a PTA president.

It's a gourmet cook.

It's Supermom!

Surely you've run into her: the woman who really Does It All. She's at the top of her profession. She's married to a great guy who adores her. Her children are incipient Rhodes scholars—and they're well-adjusted to boot.

What's more, she always seems happy, easygoing, yet in control. She always looks perfectly put together. For goodness' sake, she's even thin.

Awful how she makes you feel, isn't it? Just when you think you're doing as much as one woman possibly can, you encounter her and think: I could be doing more. I should be doing more. I will do more . . .

Stop fretting!

In case you missed it, sometime in the late 1980s, Supermom was declared a MYTH. Feminists and nonfeminists alike adopted a new battle cry: "You Can't Do It All." The newsmagazines all carried the story.

Admittedly, none of the articles bothered to explain those wonder-women we all know, those living myths. They never told us, for instance, how to account for Jane Pauley. Or for that handful of *Fortune* 500 executives who are crashing through the glass ceiling. Or for that woman in your office who's been promoted seven times since the first of her three children was born two and a half years ago.

But there's got to be some explanation. Here are a couple:

- Supermom is really identical twins. While one Supermom bounds out of bed at 4:30 A.M. to put in a half-hour of calisthenics before she cooks her family a hot breakfast, the other burrows deeper under the covers for much-needed rest. It isn't until Supermom #1 takes a lunch break that Supermom #2's day begins—vacuuming the Levolors, whipping up a *paella* and some *zabaglione* for dinner, getting out the PTA newsletter. Supermom #1 falls into bed the second she gets home from work, but at midnight Supermom #2 is still hot to trot. No wonder her husband loves her so much.
- There's only one of her, but she's bionic. Remember *The Stepford Wives*? Sure it's science fiction, but sci-fi has an eerie way of coming true. So maybe she's a Stepford Mom, built for the 1990s, hardware by Olivetti, software by IBM. She's functioning on a 640-ram mainframe with a 1.9-billion-megabyte memory and 7-way modem. Remember last summer, when she seemed a bit run-down, then took a two-day "vacation" and came back recharged? That trip to the mountains was just a ruse. She was really in the shop getting her hard drive repaired.

You say all that's implausible? Perhaps. Here's another theory:

■ Supermom isn't so super after all. In reality, she's a high-functioning neurotic overachiever. She's the kind of woman who is never, ever satisfied with ANYTHING. She's always striving for some unattainable degree of PERFECTION. She still has angst about the time she put bottled mayonnaise in her New Potato Salad.

(You like this one, huh? Let's keep going.)

Supermom is so anxiety-ridden that she shrieks at her husband and kids whenever she sees them. (Psst—it isn't often!) That's why they're so compliant and adoring: They're under her evil spell. She's so totally overwrought that she can't relax long enough to eat. That's why she's thin. Maybe she looks great, but her health is shot. She'll succumb to malnourishment. Or a massive coronary. With any luck, it will be really soon. . . .

Of course, there's the possibility that this theory isn't the right one either. What if—just what if?—there really is a Supermom. What if she's like you, only MORE COMPETENT, CAPABLE, ORGANIZED—MORE SUPER? What can you do about it?

You could try to be just like her, but you know better. Remember the last time you tried to Do It All? You had to take to your bed for a week.

You could resign yourself to the view that, much like high cheekbones, Supermomism is determined by genetics. Some women come by it naturally. You don't.

You could decide that being a Supermom is passé, like miniskirts and bell-bottoms (which, come to think of it, are making a comeback).

Or you could look up the story in the newsmagazines. It's right there in black and white: You can't do it all. Nobody can. Not even HER. Supermom is a MYTH.

ARE YOU A SUPERMOM?

1. *Since having children, my career has* _____

A. Taken off. Being a mom has enhanced my managerial and organizational abilities and I've advanced even more quickly than I anticipated.

B. Remained stable. I haven't accomplished as much as I once hoped, but, for now, I don't really mind.

C. Career? You mean my job? I'm lucky I still have it.

2. *When I come home from work, I am greeted by* _____

A. My smiling children looking forward to our special hour of "quality time."

B. My fussy, hungry kids whose main use for me is to referee their latest round of sibling rivalry.

C. A flying Lego.

3. *In my spare time, I* _____

A. Take home-baked cookies to the local nursing home.

B. Take my twenty-two-month-old to the pediatrician for his eighteen-month checkup.

C. Take a shower.

4. *To make the dinner hour smooth and easy, I generally* ___

A. Prepare and freeze a week's worth of healthy and nutritious meals every Sunday after church.

B. Reheat yesterday's Chinese take-out in the microwave.

C. Let my husband know I have to work late.

5. *My children's dresser drawers typically contain* _____
A. Comfortable clothing in natural fibers.
B. A mishmash of outfits ranging from size 2T to 14.
C. A dead goldfish.

SCORING: For each A answer, give yourself 100 points. For each B, give yourself 50 points. For each C, give yourself one point. If your score is:

0–5   You aren't Supermom.
6–498   You still aren't Supermom.
Above 499 You are Supermom. Big deal.
               You probably don't have any friends.

CHAPTER 11
Our Old Friends

finally, it's 5 P.M.

You switch off your computer, dig out your purse and turn to your office-mate to say good-night. "Back to the real world," you say brightly. She bursts into tears.

What happened to your friendship?

At one time, the two of you could talk for hours. You suffered through her affairs. She suffered through your pregnancy. Maybe—hey, she's a good sport—she even went to a Lamaze class with you when your husband had to work late.

But your paths started to diverge the minute you became a mother. And since nothing has changed in her life—and your life is changing by the millisecond—you know it's entirely your fault. You've been feeling guilty ever since she came to visit you in the hospital and got mugged in the parking lot.

You'd like to maintain the friendship, but these days, you don't even have the time to go out for a quick drink after work. Your phone conversations always get cut short by a screaming child. The few times she's invited you to the movies, you've had to decline so you could take your son to his karate class.

But you're really eager to fit her in. So you invite her over for pizza with the kids. She says she has to clean her closets. Undeterred, you suggest lunch, and, happily, she's free. By the time you've got your salads, you've run through office politics, where she's traveling on business and how well your kids are doing in school.

In the spirit of friendship, you ask what single people are doing for Safe Sex these days. She snarls at you to mind your own business. She asks if you know any nice men who want to have children. You tell her that there are exactly two, but they're already married. She bursts into tears and races off to her therapist.

The trouble is, she thinks you've got a perfect life. And at moments when your juggling act seems especially precarious, you think she has it pretty soft.

Here's how your friend thinks you spend your Saturdays:

Your husband brings you breakfast in bed. Just as you're finishing your coffee, you hear the patter of little feet. The kids snuggle with you. While your little family does the breakfast dishes, you take a long shower. Then you go out together for a long walk and a picnic. In the afternoon, while the kids nap simultaneously for two hours, you and your husband make love. After a cozy family dinner, your husband bathes the kids who, sweet-smelling in their pajamas, pad downstairs to kiss you goodnight. Before your own bedtime, your husband reads Dickens aloud while you sew.

And here's how you think your friend spends her Saturdays:

Her lover brings her breakfast in bed. They have two hours of passionate sex, including one hour of foreplay. After a shared Jacuzzi, he leaves for a tennis lesson while she unpacks her suitcase from her business trip to San Francisco that week. Then she's out the door: a shopping expedition for white-on-white fabric for a new sofa. Lunch with friends and plenty of wine. A visit to the new Picasso exhibition and, unscheduled, coffee with Paolo, an Italian sculptor she bumps into at the art museum. An exercise class. Dinner at the trendiest new restaurant with her lover. And home to bed, for two hours of passionate sex, including a complete body massage.

Pretty nice, huh?

The only thing wrong with these pictures is that they don't have any basis in fact. In the back of your mind, you know that. But maybe your friend needs to be convinced. You invite her over for dinner and a dose of Reality.

This time, she comes, bearing gifts for the kids. Conversation lags because you had only four hours of sleep (your toddler was sick) and she had five hours (she stayed up to watch David Letterman after a bad date). It doesn't really matter, because the children are so noisy you can barely think. It's one of those days where you think of instituting grace before dinner just to have a minute of silence.

The meal is an unmitigated disaster. You put the burritos in the microwave for six minutes instead of sixty seconds and they taste like spicy rubber. Your two-year-old fingerpaints with the guacamole. Your son tries to impress your friend with the latest moron joke he heard on the playground. Against your better judgment, you laugh; your girlfriend gets indigestion.

By the end of the evening, everybody's the wiser. She leaves with an audible sigh of relief that she doesn't have children. When the door closes behind her, you breathe a sigh of relief that you're not returning to her (by your terms) empty apartment. You decide that, on balance, you prefer the chaos. And for that small satisfaction—admit it!—you feel a little bit guilty.

FRIENDSHIPS: BEFORE AND AFTER

WE USED TO LOOK FOR FRIENDS WHO . . .	WE NOW LOOK FOR FRIENDS WHO . . .
Were footloose and fancy-free	Are grounded with at least two kids
Entertained with elegant dinner parties for eight	Entertain with potluck suppers and backyard barbecues
Shared a passion for the same sports	Share the same soccer schedule
Lived in a house with a gourmet kitchen	Live in a house with a basement playroom
Drove a hot foreign sports car with leather interior	Drive a four-door minivan with upholstery that doesn't show stains
Would let us use their sailboat	Will let us use their camcorder
Could set us up with a respectable date	Can set us up with a responsible baby-sitter
Knew the best place to shop for designer clothes	Know the best place to shop for consignment clothes

CHAPTER 12

The Television Moms

Those of us who grew up in the 1950s and 1960s received our images of motherhood mainly through cathode rays. As a result, we grew up believing that kids spent most of their free time building cars for the Soap Box Derby, dads showed them how to do it—and moms provided the soapboxes.

Now that we're grown up, we know that life isn't what we see on television. Still, those airwave images die hard.

'Fess up. How many times have you found yourself wishing that your sons shared a bedroom as peaceably as Beaver and Wally Cleaver? That your house—not to mention your hairdo—was as impeccable as Donna Reed's? That your blended family was as happy-go-lucky as the Brady Bunch?

Fortunately, as the medium has matured, Television Moms have gotten a bit more true to life. Now we've had Hope Steadman of *thirtysomething* who's as conflicted as we are about kids and career and probably a lot more whiny; and Roseanne Barr, who reminds us that, no matter how bad things seem, they could always be worse.

But, just for the fun of it, let's think back to the Television Moms of yesteryear. Here's a trivia test to determine how deeply they've invaded your psyche.

1. Can you name the three well-adjusted, well-behaved children of the devoted fifties homemaker who didn't mind publicly acknowledging that Father Knows Best? You get extra points if you remember their nicknames.
2. What television mother consistently offered milk and cookies as a solution to her two sons' little problems, or alternatively, sent them to talk to their dad for a moralistic lesson about life?

3. What kind of work did Donna Reed's husband do that allowed the family to live so comfortably on one income?

4. What fifties Television Mom was married to a man—both on-screen and off—whose real name was worse than her own?

5. While we're on the subject of awful names, who was Donna Reed's neighbor who fueled the stereotype that sixties housewives engaged in idle gossip?

6. Why was Ward Cleaver so boring?

7. Who played Laura, a ditsy but delightful sixties housewife who was married to Rob Petrie and had one son, Richie?

8. (Fill in the blanks.) I would happily put up with a meddlesome mother, a nerdy husband whose boss frequently came to dinner and Gladys Kravitz if I were a _____ like _____ .

9. Who was one of television's first Working Mothers who had a job that allowed her to travel around the country in an old painted school bus with her children? (Bonus question: What was the major drawback of her job?)

10. Name the daffy housekeeper on *The Brady Bunch* whose presence enabled Carol Brady to be sensitive, patient and forbearing not only with her own children, but with her stepchildren as well?

ANSWERS:

1. The children of Jim and Margaret Anderson were Betty, James Jr. and Kathy, endearingly referred to as Princess, Bud and Kitten. Cute, eh?

2. June Cleaver, who, by the way, wore prim cotton dresses, high heels, a pearl necklace and presumably an all-in-one bra and girdle while vacuuming the house. If you have any idea why, you've already passed this test.

3. Dr. Alex Stone was a pediatrician who evidently made good money. On the down side, he worked in the days when doctors still made house calls and was always running out of the house at odd hours.

4. Harriet Nelson, who, with husband Ozzie, had the good sense to choose names like Rick and David for their kids.
5. Midge. When was the last time you heard anyone called that?
6. Because he was an accountant.
7. Mary Tyler Moore on *The Dick Van Dyke Show*. Moore later went on to play a ditsy but delightful TV newswriter who had no husband or kids, perpetuating the old notion that one is either a mother or a career woman, not both.
8. Witch, Samantha. In fact, it's fairly certain that if you had Sam's powers for even an hour a week, your life would be a lot more manageable.
9. Shirley Partidge. (Bonus answer: Having to sing "I Think I Love You" four trillion times.)
10. Alice Nelson. Okay, maybe she was loony, but betcha you wouldn't mind her doing your dishes every night.

PART FOUR

The Guilt Amplifiers

Some Special Situations That Increase Our Guilt

CHAPTER 13

Vacation Guilt

What every Working Mother really needs is a vacation.

Maybe a week alone at some exclusive spa where you are served exquisite, low-calorie meals and receive a separate beauty treatment for each pore.

Or maybe a week with your husband in Paris, boating down the Seine, touring museums, dining at four-star restaurants, perhaps even dancing the night away at some chic and trendy club.

As your ten-year-old son would say: "Get a Life!"

If you're like most Working Mothers, you see a vacation as a chance to spend real Quality Time with your kids. So what if you have to spend the three preceding weeks packing and the three weeks after you get home doing laundry? And so what if you spend the entire time feeling guilty that things aren't going as well as you'd hoped?

It's probably worth it.

Or is it?

A lot depends on what kind of vacation you plan. Here are some tips on finding the family vacation spot that's best for you.

AVOID . . .

Charming Country Inns—where the rooms are filled with expensive, breakable antiques and the other guests are child-loathing yuppies on a romantic fling or parents of young children who had the good sense to leave them home with a baby-sitter.

Glamorous Island Resorts—where flat-stomached women in bikinis— obviously not mothers—lounge on the beach and are unlikely to welcome the stares of a pubescent twelve-year-old who's never seen cleavage like that before.

The Continent of Europe—where you will spend large numbers of your weak American dollars to expose your child to history, culture and fine cuisine—and all that will impress him will be chain-pull toilets at the Louvre.

Rugged Outdoor Adventures—like white-water rafting, where anything weighing less than 50 pounds has a 95 percent likelihood of being tossed from the boat and forever lost to a Class III rapid.

Exotic Developing Countries—where your children run the risk of coming down with cholera on the one occasion they decide to brush their teeth without your reminding them.

INSTEAD, OPT FOR . . .

Big Chain Hotels—where all families with kids are sequestered on one noisy floor and you don't have to feel bad that your youngsters are racing up and down the halls screaming, because if they weren't doing it, someone else's would be.

Large Theme Parks—with high entrance fees, lousy food, long lines, stomach-churning rides and the opportunity to spend an entire week's salary on T-shirts, barrettes and bedsheets featuring Saturday-morning cartoon-show characters.

Rustic Cabins or Campgrounds—where you'll be able to spend lots of time with the kids while you smear them with sunscreen, check them for ticks carrying Lyme disease and cook them three (instead of the usual two) meals a day—without the aid of a microwave or dishwasher.

Dude Ranches or Working Farms—where the kids get plenty of fresh air and wholesome food, fall asleep immediately after dinner and get to say words like "bitch" and "tit" with impunity.

Grandma's House.

HOW I SPENT MY SUMMER VACATION
By Karen Devaney

Before we had kids, Bob and I had always enjoyed camping. So last summer, we decided we'd try it as a family. We all had a wonderful time, except for a few small problems.

Our plan was to leave on Friday night, right after work, but since we couldn't find Nora's other sneaker until midnight, we pulled out first thing Saturday. It was just as well, because the trip took longer than we'd expected. We had to make a U-turn on the interstate when Nora threw her teddy bear out of the car. And it would have been kind of scary for the kids if we'd run out of gas in the dark instead of at noon.

I'd forgotten how dark it can get in the countryside at night. As soon as we set up the tent, Josh demanded his night light, and when we pointed to the Big Dipper, he said it wasn't bright enough. He said he was afraid of bears, scorpions and dinosaurs. I told him the Wisconsin Dells had nothing but cows, but he said he was afraid of them, too. Anyway, he fell asleep with the flashlight on, which was fine except it seemed to keep Nora awake.

Nora, on the other hand, turned out to be a natural for camping. At times she might even have been a little too enthusiastic. The first night, when her marshmallow fell off her stick, she nearly followed it into the campfire. After that, we shopped for dinner at the 7-Eleven.

The lake was another problem, but luckily both Bob and I had taken a course in CPR that included mouth-to-mouth resuscitation. And she wasn't under very long, either time.

I'm sure Josh would have learned to love camping, too, if the weather had been better. It tends to be on the sultry side in August, so we certainly hadn't expected a tornado warning. Even so, it probably would have seemed like a great adventure, if it hadn't started in the middle of the night and we couldn't see to break camp because the flashlight battery was dead. After that, we checked into a motel.

The kids loved the motel, but by then Nora was coming down with a bad ear infection, maybe from all that time in the lake. At least that was the opinion of the pediatrician at the all-night clinic we found around 3:00 A.M. It's great that you can find a doctor at that hour, and it would have been perfect if only they'd accepted our health insurance.

Between the motel and the clinic, we'd used up the last of our cash, so we decided to head for home. It was an easy trip back and, although I always worry about Josh getting carsick, he managed to hold it until we had almost pulled into our driveway. I told him I was very proud of him.

Anyway, it was a great trip, and the best part of it was that when I called the office to let them know we'd returned a week early, they told me to come on in.

HOW I SPENT MY WINTER VACATION
by Karen Devaney

After our family camping trip last summer, Bob and I agreed that we needed a break from the kids. So when winter rolled around and my mom said she could take Josh and Nora for a long weekend, we headed off to Miami for fun in the sun.

I have to admit I was a little anxious. Maybe more than a little. For one thing, Bob and I hadn't been alone together since Josh was born, unless you count the time I was in labor with Nora, and, even then, the nurses kept popping in every few minutes.

For another, the second the plane took off, I remembered we'd never gotten around to making wills or naming guardians for the kids. For the next three hours I kept a lookout for small aircraft

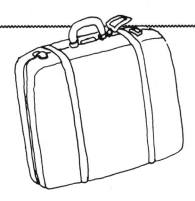

and rehearsed the instructions for emergency landings over water. Once I got the plane on the runway, I felt a lot better, and after Bob and I checked into our hotel room, we felt a whole lot better.

Everything was great until I put on my bathing suit. For the last few years, we've been going to a neighborhood pool where there's nobody between the ages of five and thirty-five, and even the men look like they've had a baby or two. I'd forgotten about teenage girls. Luckily, the hotel had enormous towels, and once I was waist-deep in the water I felt safe.

Probably too safe. By the time I edged out of the water and found my towel, I was pretty sunburned. The hotel doctor gave me a shot and told me to keep out of the sun. He gave me some antibiotics, too, for the bladder infection I'd developed as a result of my little romp with Bob, and suggested that I refrain from intercourse. I hadn't heard the word intercourse in years.

After that, there wasn't much I could do, so I kept phoning home. I also kept thinking of what my neighbor, who's also a Working Mother, says about vacations: "I see it as a time for a family to be a family." That made me feel bad because there I was, finally, with some time to be a family, and we'd left the kids at home. Oh well, I never liked that neighbor anyway.

I spent the rest of the time shopping for souvenirs. We bought a lobster bib for Nora and swim trunks for Josh in Day-Glo pink and green that could look pretty strange in Milwaukee. We got both kids "My parents went to Miami and all I got was this lousy T-shirt" T-shirts. We bought my mother a crystal vase.

On the return flight, I picked up $2 million in air travel insurance. If Josh and Nora were going to be orphans, at least they'd be rich orphans! But we made it back. The kids were busy watching TV and didn't look up. But my mom flung herself into our arms.

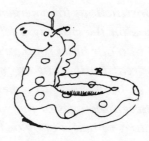

C H A P T E R   1 4

Holiday Guilt

Christmas couldn't come soon enough when you were a kid—and the same was true of Thanksgiving, Halloween, the Fourth of July and, for the matter, any holiday at all.

But now that you've got children of your own, the holidays seem to come all too soon. Each time one comes around, you recall the way you used to celebrate holidays, and you start making plans. Then reality sets in.

Here's a look at why Christmas isn't necessarily the season to be jolly:

WHAT WE'D LIKE TO BE DOING	WHAT WE CONCEIVABLY COULD BE DOING	WHAT WE WILL ACTUALLY BE DOING
Strolling through decorated department stores carefully selecting appropriate gifts while humming "Silent Night."	Ordering Christmas presents from catalogs in October, and gift wrapping them as soon as they arrive.	Racing through the aisles of Toys Я Us, which, fortunately, stays open until midnight the week before Christmas.
Rolling, cutting and decorating cookies with our children, to give as gifts to teachers, crossing guards and baby-sitters.	Making cookies with the refrigerated cookie dough sold in the dairy case. (Check the wrapper for quick decorating tips!)	Buying cookies at a bakery and arranging them on a paper plate to take to our son's holiday recital, where we've been asked to bring something homemade.
Volunteering to serve Christmas Eve dinner at the local homeless shelter.	Writing a check for fifty dollars and sending it to our favorite charity.	Stuffing our last dollar bill into the Salvation Army bell-ringer's bucket as we race out of the mall.
Driving to the country to cut our own white spruce Christmas tree and decorating it with popcorn-and-cranberry chains strung by our children.	Buying a Christmas tree from the local Boy Scout troop and letting each of the children buy one special decoration to hang on it.	Giving our kids candy canes to keep them quiet while we decorate the tree with what's left of last year's ornaments.
Inviting our extended family for a traditional, home-cooked meal on Christmas afternoon.	Organizing a potluck Christmas supper with friends and family.	Eating Christmas dinner at our mother-in-law's.

HOLIPHOBIAS

Suddenly, Halloween is giving you the kind of goose bumps you haven't had since you were a kid. And that's not the only scary holiday. In fact, every holiday has its own special terrors, because every holiday raises expectations that you—as an overworked Working Mother—probably won't be able to meet. And that's the perfect prescription for Guilt.

Here are some of the fears you might experience as each holiday looms:

New Year's Eve—That you won't be able to get a baby-sitter. Or, worse still, that you will get a sitter at a premium price, then go out to a party and fall asleep at 10:30 P.M.

Valentine's Day—That you will spend the night before coaxing, threatening and begging your child to write her name on twenty-four valentines, then end up doing it yourself after she's gone to bed.

Presidents' Day—That, now that they've done away with the individual holidays, you won't remember which Great American Leaders are being feted and will tell your child you're honoring the presidents of all the department stores.

Easter—That you'll forget to buy the eggs or the dye or both and that your kids, charged up on jelly beans, will spend the entire holiday hunting under couch cushions and inside cluttered closets before you have the courage to admit that the Easter bunny overslept. Again.

Passover—That your child will interpret the word "recline" literally and insist on lying down for the entire Seder.

Mother's Day—That your children will bring you breakfast in bed at 6 A.M.

Father's Day—That you will have to shop for a tie or socks that your kids can give their dad, and, even worse, that you'll have to let him take the day off.

Fourth of July—That your older child will sleep through the fireworks that he desperately wanted to see, while the noise will wake up your baby, who will spend the rest of the night in tears.

Halloween—That every child on the block will be dressed as Snow White, Little Red Riding Hood or Peter Pan in a handmade costume and your child will be disguised as a ball of string.

Thanksgiving—That you will forget to reserve a fresh turkey at the butcher's, then neglect to thaw the frozen one you bought at the supermarket and end up having to serve spaghetti and meatballs.

Hanukkah—That you will run out of ideas and presents by the third of eight days of gift-giving, and wind up giving things you pocketed on your last overnight business trip, like shower caps and small sewing kits.

Christmas—That even Santa will reject the store-bought cookies you set out for him next to the chimney.

Your Child's Birthday—That you won't be able to come up with an original idea for his birthday party ("Aww c'mon, Mom, I've been to six pirate parties already this year") and so will end up taking twenty-five kids to Chuck E. Cheese, where you'll lose your mind and maybe even someone else's child.

CHAPTER 15

Bonus Guilt: Single, Step and Adoptive Mothers

Your kid won't eat his peas.

It's probably because you're a Single Mom.

Intellectually, of course, you know that has nothing to do with it. No kids eat peas, not even ones with a mom, a dad, a little sister and a dog named Spot. But every time something goes wrong—when your child's ornery, when he won't go to bed at night or get up in the morning, when he catches a cold, when he won't learn to read—you immediately assume it's because he doesn't have a father.

All right, so he does have a father. Maybe he even has a Devoted Dad who demands alternate weekends and half the summer. Who calls every night for a meaningful conversation when, really, all your kid wants to do is watch TV. Who bombards your child with useless but large and expensive presents every holiday, including Groundhog Day.

Maybe he even has a father who sends monthly child support payments on time. Or at least lies convincingly when he says the check is in the mail.

But in your mind, this kind of dad is not the Real Thing. No matter how you look at it, there's no adult male in your household, unless you count the dog, and you had him fixed last month. So—of course—your kid won't eat his peas.

EVEN if he did eat his peas, though—and make straight A's at school, and clean his room, and say "Yes, Mother" instead of "Do I have to, Maaaa?"—the going would still be rough. Being a Single Working Mother is hard work.

But if you must say so yourself—and you MUST, since there's no one else around to say so—you're managing pretty nicely. In fact, you're doing a great job.

You never let any negative feelings about your child's father slip out. You sing his praises so convincingly that you sometimes wonder why you left the guy in the first place.

You do your best to inject a Male Presence into your child's life. You seek out professional men as role models: a male pediatrician (a dying breed), a dentist, the grocery store cashier. (So what if the male checkout clerks always seem to have the longest line?) You find a day-care center staffed with Nurturing Males. You urge your friends and relatives to bring husbands and Significant Others along when they come to visit. You've been so insistent, in fact, that some malicious types have begun suggesting you want a man for yourself.

And maybe you do. You could use a little companionship. Okay, maybe that's an understatement. There have been moments lately when you've been considering marrying the first person who tests HIV-negative.

BUT in your saner moments, you realize that marriage would mean an end to the cozy little family you've created. Introduce a man into the household, and in no time at all, he'd be making demands. He'd ask for space in the closet—and there's barely enough room for the two of you. He'd expect you to cook food that he likes. He'd want to sit next to you in the car—he might even want to drive the car! He'd probably try to engage you in conversation. And in the morning, when your kid crawls into bed with you to snuggle, he'd be in the way.

And besides, how could anyone possibly love your child as much as you do?

So you focus on the bright side of your harried but happy life. You remind yourself that, since you don't have a husband, you can fantasize about Richard Gere—without having to wake up to the reality of somebody who doesn't measure up. There's always enough hot water for a shower, and you never have to paw through the towel rack to find one that's dry.

The laundry's lighter, and so are the groceries—no six-packs of beer to lug home. After the kid is in bed, you can watch whatever video you want. You can't be expected to drive the baby-sitter home. There's no mother-in-law.

Scheduling is simpler, too. You never have to check the calendar to see whose turn it is to pick up your kid from day-care.

Baby, it's you.

AN EXCERPT FROM *PEOPLE* MAGAZINE'S "HERO" COLUMN

A Single Mother by Choice, Gutsy Rhoda Siegel is Winner of MacArthur Award for Guilt Management

Four years ago, when then-forty-two-year-old Rhoda Siegel gave birth, even her closest friends were shocked. First of all, the twice-divorced New Yorker had kept her pregnancy a secret by moving to Queens for the last trimester. Then there was the fact that Siegel hadn't had a date in more than a year.

What her friends didn't know was that, nine months before, Siegel, then an advertising copywriter, had visited a sperm bank. "I was able to screen the potential donors for things that were really important," she says. Of the unknown father, she notes, "We're both Libras."

While Siegel says she's been blissfully happy since the birth of little Matthew, she started noticing that other women in her situation were plagued by guilt. "Whenever things went wrong, they had no one to blame but a turkey baster," she says. "That wasn't enough."

Not one to sit idly by, she formed a support group, Just Moms. Now there are chapters in New York, Los Angeles and San Francisco, and plans for more. Last week the MacArthur Foundation, which awards "genius" grants in a variety of fields, recognized Siegel's work in guilt management with a $25,000 annual stipend for life.

As a child in Flatbush, N.Y., Rhoda, the daughter of a sanitation engineer and a dental hygienist, learned to take matters into her own hands. During one of New York's periodic subway strikes, she sold lemonade on the Brooklyn Bridge to foot-sore commuters. Still the entrepreneur, a year ago she formed her own advertising agency, Siegel, Puleo, with another single mom.

Now that Siegel's dating record-company executive Allan Herbert, there are signs her single life could change. But she insists she won't abandon her mission to ease the burden of guilt on single working moms. And in the meantime, the MacArthur award will go a long way to paying Matthew's preschool tuition.

THE WICKED STEPMOTHER

As a Stepmother, any extra guilt you've got probably stems from the fact that, subliminally, you worry that you're wicked. This notion comes from some outdated, sexist fairy tale that, by the way, is still raking in zillions for Walt Disney's stockholders.

All it's doing for you, however, is making you believe that Stepmothers are intrinsically evil. So whenever anything goes wrong in your "blended family," you blame yourself.

Are you really wicked? Take this quick quiz to find out if you're any match for Cinderella's or Snow White's Stepmother.

Your husband-to-be suggests bringing his two children along on your honeymoon. You:

A. Welcome the opportunity as a chance to bond with your new blended family. After all, the honeymoon suite you've booked is plenty big for four.
B. Suggest as an alternative that you take a second family "honeymoon" to Walt Disney World next spring.
C. Agree, knowing full well that the kids can't stand you and will never consent to come along.

Your stepchildren call you:

A. "Mom," because, after all, that's what you're trying to be.
B. Either by your first name or by some endearing nickname such as LuLu, if your real name is Lucy.
C. Expletives that you'd prefer not to repeat.

You attend an art exhibition at your stepdaughter's school. Amid countless portraits of traditional American families, you can easily pick out the one she's drawn because:

A. It depicts her in the middle with her mom on one side, and you and her father on the other. Everyone is wearing big, bright smiles.
B. Her name is on the bottom. Other than that, her drawing is the same as everyone else's. It shows her mom, her dad, her brother and herself. You've been left out.
C. The drawing depicts everyone in her entire extended and blended family, including a great-grandmother who's the same age as you, an aunt who is eleven, a half-brother-in-law's cousin, and assorted

children and pets. You're in there, too, but you're crammed in beside a pit bull you've never seen and you're wearing a pointed black hat.

You and your husband decide to punish his teenager for a grave misdeed by forbidding him to leave the house during his weekend visit. You overhear your stepson tell his friends, "My stepmother grounded me." The tone is so disparaging that he might as well have inserted the adjective "wicked." You react by:

A. Sitting down and having a meaningful discussion with him that leads to a warm, happy mutual embrace.
B. Reminding yourself that the adjustment has been hard on the boy, but shedding a few tears nonetheless.
C. Buying a bulletproof vest, anticipating his next move.

Which best describes your feelings about your stepchildren as compared to your own children:

A. "I love them as dearly as I love my own."
B. "Of course my feelings toward my own children are stronger, but with each passing day, I grow closer to my stepchildren."
C. "Considering how horribly they've been treating me, I'd rather not tell you how I feel about them right now."

SCORING: For each A answer, give yourself 5 poisoned apples. For each B, give yourself 10 poisoned apples. For each C, 15 poisoned apples. If your score is:

0–25 You probably are not wicked, but you probably are lying, since no blended family blends that smoothly.

25–50 You're not wicked at all. In fact, you're probably a very wonderful Stepmom, Cinderella be damned.

50–75 You're probably not wicked, but your stepchildren clearly think you are. Don't despair; these relationships take time.

117

ADOPTIVE MOTHER GUILT

For all purposes, practical and otherwise, an Adoptive Mother is no different from a biological mom. Whether you first saw your baby in the hospital delivery room or at the airport waiting area, the feelings you have for him are the same.

But when it comes to guilt, as a mother of an adoptive child, you have a few more things you can add to the list. If you're an Adoptive Mom, you may feel guilty that . . .

- You didn't endure nine months of pregnancy and twelve hours of labor, but instead got the baby the easy way—after five years of infertility treatments, dozens of interviews with adoption agencies and a $25,000 payment to a lawyer.
- You took the baby away from the beautiful mountains of Chile (or Tennessee or Oregon or Korea) to be raised in Secaucus, where the standard of living may be higher, but so are the rates of cancer and crime.
- You've separated your child from his biological family—eleven warm and loving siblings and an energetic, young (read, teenage) mother who would still have the baby strapped to her back instead of in day-care.
- You haven't yet told your child that she's adopted, even though she's started to say "mama" and understands words like "bottle."
- You're not raising him Taoist or fundamentalist or whatever his parents were, but Congregationalist and probably in the wrong political party, too.
- You spend hours studying the baby to see whether she's starting to look like you.
- You said "Thank you" when somebody said, "What a beautiful baby." And when somebody else wondered how you, a brown-eyed brunette, could have produced a child with blond hair and blue eyes, you snapped, "He takes after his father," then gleefully watched the busybody's bewilderment deepen when your brown-eyed, brown-haired husband showed up.

PART FIVE

The Guilt-Free

CHAPTER 16

Why Men Don't Feel Guilty

(WITH APOLOGIES TO THE HALF-DOZEN WHO DO)

Oh, lucky you.

It's Saturday morning, and your husband has offered to take care of the kids while you sleep. You pull your pillow over your head to muffle the noises from downstairs, and catch up on some much needed rest.

Two hours later, you awaken and head down to . . . disaster. Your husband has made pancakes for breakfast—but he hasn't cleaned up. He's allowed the kids to pull every toy out of the toybox—but he hasn't reminded them to put them back. He's dressed the children—but your daughter's playsuit is on backwards and your son is wearing the sneakers he outgrew six months ago.

You're tempted to scream, "IS THIS YOUR IDEA OF TAKING CARE OF THE KIDS?" But just as the words start to form, you bite your tongue.

You know that if you criticize him now, he may never do it again. Besides, he's standing there smiling, looking so totally and completely proud of himself.

REAL men eat quiche. Real men cry. Real men are nurturing fathers. So why don't real men feel guilty that they're not doing a Perfect Job when it comes to taking care of their kids?

That is the question for the nineties.

Now that women are doing practically everything that men do, why aren't men doing anywhere near everything that women do? And, since they're not Doing It All—or for that matter, even one-quarter of It All —why don't they feel guilty?

It's a well-established fact that men don't feel guilt. Scratch a man (Psst—he'll love it!) and you won't find a particle of guilt beneath that furry exterior. If you've got any doubts, ask him why he doesn't feel bad that he's not doing more. Chances are he'll look genuinely bewildered. Maybe he'll say he's doing plenty and you just don't notice. Maybe he'll have the gall to say he would do even more, only you do it first. "Doing more?" he might say. "I do more than my father ever did."

Aaaah. So that's the answer!

You've been comparing yourself with your mother, whose kitchen floor you could eat off (but never did because the table was always set). And your mate has been comparing himself with his father, who in all likelihood didn't do a damn thing.

Okay, maybe the old guy took out the garbage. That's macho. And maybe he even "helped out" by vacuuming the carpet when "company" was coming. But that's only because vacuuming was noisy and mechanical and probably phallic, and the "company" couldn't see him doing it.

The trouble is, though, it's not 1958 anymore. You've got kids and a job and monthly mortgage payments that are probably more than what your parents paid for their entire house. And you've got a husband who seems a little lost in a Time Warp.

Oddly enough, though, in most other respects, he's a Thoroughly Modern Man. He was a gourmet cook before you got married and, with one whiff, he can still tell you've put too much thyme in the sauce. But he can't smell a dirty diaper until after you've taken it off the baby. He can program his computer to pick the Super Bowl team for the year 2000, yet he can't notice that you're running low on milk. His hearing is kind of erratic, too; he's already telling you he really needs to trade in the CD player for a digital-audio tapedeck, but he can sleep through the kids' most bloodcurdling nightmares

So with Robert Young as a role model and a sensory system as delicate as a Mack truck, how could he feel guilty?

What's worse, it doesn't look like he ever will. "Sensitive men," who were so trendy in the seventies, today are called "wimps." The latest men's movement, this Iron John business, is big on feelings—but manly feelings. When the gurus rhapsodize about men communing with nature, they're not talking about hanging out the wash. When the gurus say men need to connect more with their fathers, they probably mean taking out the garbage.

So what's a Working Mother to do?

You might attempt to "raise his consciousness," even though the term is kind of passé. Do it subtly. Leave some pertinent reading material in the bathroom, like *The Sociology of Housework*, *Women and Madness*, the directions for cleaning the oven. But chances are, he'll brush it all aside and pick up *Sports Illustrated*.

Or you could try going on strike and doing nothing at all. Wait for him to notice that your baby has outgrown all her T-shirts; that you're completely out of diapers; that the kids' school medical forms are three weeks overdue. The trouble is, by the time he's aware something is amiss, the child welfare people could be at your door—and they'll be screaming at you.

Or you might try shock therapy. Walk out the door for a week, and he'd have to become domesticated, right? In the movies, it works every time. With your luck, though, it wouldn't. Somebody—his mother, your mother, your best friend—would feel sorry for him and hurry over to take charge.

Well, things could be worse.

You could be married to a complete cad who never once offers to take care of the kids while you sleep. Or you could be not married at all. And some slightly inept man in the house is certainly better than none.

So consider yourself lucky that you're married to a nice guy, a loving companion, a caring father . . . not to mention a man you can usually count on, at the very least, to take out the garbage.

A QUIZ FOR YOUR HUSBAND: ARE YOU GUILTY?

INSTRUCTIONS: NEXT TO EACH QUESTION, PUT "Y" for yes or "N" for no. STOP AT THE END OF EACH SECTION.

PART ONE:
Have you ever:

1. Changed your baby's diapers? _____

2. Given your kids a bath? _____

3. Gotten up in the middle of the night to tend to a crying child? _____

4. Taken your child to the pediatrician? _____

5. Spent an afternoon alone with the kids while your spouse went out? _____

6. Rearranged your work schedule because of child-related considerations? _____

STOP HERE!

If you've answered yes to all of the above questions, you may be patting yourself on the back. NOT SO QUICK, BUDDY. This isn't 1958. The purpose of this section was simply to show you how this test works. It also was intended to screen out any Hopeless Cases. If you answered "no" to even one of the above questions, you can stop here, you Guilt-Free Male Chauvinist Pig. For the rest of you guys, continue to the next section.

PART TWO:
Have you ever:

1. Bought clothing for your children? (T-shirts with the name of your alma mater, favorite sports team or employer DO NOT APPLY!) _____

2. Realized that your son has outgrown his sneakers and taken him out to buy new ones—completely on your own initiative? _____

3. Called your spouse from the office and said, "Honey, I'll be a few minutes late getting home. I just remembered we're running low on milk, and I'm going to stop to pick some up." _____

4. Planned and executed a child's birthday party with minimal help from your spouse? _____

5. Sorted, washed, dried, folded and put away family laundry—in less than a three-day period—without any help or prompting from your spouse? _____

6. Organized a car pool to your toddler's preschool and done car-pool duty at least as often as your spouse has but probably more? _____

STOP HERE!

Okay, now we're getting down to the nitty-gritty. Before scoring yourself on this section, ask your wife to take the same test. If your "no's" exceed hers, you have good reason to feel guilty (even though you probably don't). If you and she have an equal number of "no" answers, you should proceed to Part Three.

PART THREE:

Have you ever:

1. Felt a sharp pang in your heart as you watched your child run happily into the arms of his baby-sitter while you went off to work?   ———

2. Called home during the day because you had a gut feeling your child was about to smother himself with a plastic dry cleaner's bag?   ———

3. Offered to bake cookies for a class party even though you were swamped with work, because you were afraid that if you brought store-bought ones people might think you're too busy for your kids?   ———

4. Agonized over the possibility that you weren't giving your child enough help with his homework—or that you were doing too much of it yourself—because you were preoccupied with your job?   ———

5. Taken a day off work after an out-of-town trip because you wanted to make sure you hadn't damaged your relationship with your child?   ———

6. Considered cutting back on your work hours—or quitting work completely—because you worried that your child needed more of your time?   ———

If you've answered yes to three or more of the above questions, congratulations! You are one of the world's half-dozen Guilty Working Fathers.

A CONVERSATION WITH THE DEVIL'S ADVOCATE
About Guilt-Free Fathers

DEVIL'S ADVOCATE: Do you really want men to feel guilty?

WORKING MOTHER: Why not? I feel ten times guiltier than my husband does. And I do ten times more! Why couldn't he feel just a twinge of guilt every now and then?

DEVIL'S ADVOCATE: I wonder if you've really thought about what that would mean. Imagine what it would be like for your husband. Suddenly he starts feeling guilty about the fact that he puts in more hours on the tennis court than in the kitchen. You know how fragile he is—he'd probably have to go to bed for a week. And how would that make you feel?

WORKING MOTHER: (Sighs) Guilty.

DEVIL'S ADVOCATE: Exactly. So why not leave well enough alone?

WORKING MOTHER: Hmmm, a good point. . . .

DEVIL'S ADVOCATE: I thought you'd see it my way.

WORKING MOTHER: Wait a minute! Don't you work for a man?

AN EXCERPT FROM *THE NEW ENGLAND JOURNAL OF MEDICINE*

CHRONIC GUILT DEFICIENCY IN THE WORKING FATHER

Steve Sanguine, M.D., and
Ova Whelmed, Ph.D.

INTRODUCTION

Macho Cojones and colleagues in Spain were the first to describe the clinical appearance in working fathers of self-satisfaction and delusional thought processes regarding their involvement in child-rearing. They reported an equal distribution for class and age. Intellectual development and hair growth were variable. Annoying habits were typical. Sexual maturation occurred normally, i.e., hardly ever. Since the reports from Cojones, subjects have been described in reports from France[1], Mexico[2], Israel[3], Saudi Arabia[4], Italy[5] and Japan[6]. The condition was originally thought to result from an absence of progesterone, which in the female is secreted at the moment of conception. However, subsequent studies have established that the adoptive mother feels acute levels of guilt similar to those found in the biological working mother.

To examine the presentation of this phenomenon in the United States, we studied 20 subjects (10 Caucasian, 6 Hispanic and 4 Afro-American), selected primarily from a large population of men at restaurants during the lunch hour. Health-club owners assisted in finding other subjects.

METHODS
Precious bodily fluids were obtained from all subjects under a protocol approved by the Women's Research Institute of Secaucus Community College. Samples were taken twice daily, when the subject left his house for the office and when he returned at the end of the working day. Samples were also sought from subjects' wives. However, because most were too busy to participate, results are invalid for statistical analysis. Subjects were also subjected to tests that included magnetic resonance imaging of the brain.

RESULTS
In all 20 subjects, MRI scans showed the rigid compartmentalization characteristic of the male brain. In addition, there was nearly complete atrophy of hindbrain regions responsible for guilt, and a compensatory hypertrophy of primitive cortical structures responsible for inane sports metaphors.

To determine whether the observed clinical behavior was mediated by an immune dysfunction, we evaluated the role of estrogen and testosterone in helper T-lymphocyte function. The addition of estrogen to the media resulted in extreme nurturing activity toward young B-cell lymphocytes. However, when testosterone was combined with estrogen, the helper T-cells responded only to beer.

DISCUSSION
Research tends to support the conclusion of Cojones and other investigators that guilt deficiency in the working father is a persistent condition so prevalent that it must be deemed normal. Our results indicate that it develops in the presence of high levels of guilt in the working mother. Because further investigation would be of relevance almost exclusively to the female population, we suggest abandoning this line of investigation.

PART SIX

The Guilt Assuagers

Some of the Ridiculous Ways We Cope

CHAPTER 17

Buying Away
Our Guilt

AN EXCERPT FROM *THE WALL STREET JOURNAL*

"MATTEL MOM" IS TOYMAKERS' DOLL
Special to The Wall Street Journal

Five minutes to closing time, Karen Devaney is racing down the aisles of Toys Я Us. After a long day at the office, she has given her children their dinner, waited until her husband has come home, and slipped out to buy some toys. She grimaces guiltily as she tosses another $95 robot onto the pile in her cart. "I know I don't spend enough time with my kids," says Ms. Devaney, a marketing executive and mother of two, "so I try to make up for it by giving them things."

It is upon working mothers like Ms. Devaney that U.S. toy manufacturers such as Mattel, Hasbro and Fisher-Price are pinning their hopes this year. While mothers

who work outside the home represent 59 percent of all women with children, they account for 97.8 percent of toy purchases. In the trade, these women are known—fondly—as Mattel Moms. "If it weren't for Mattel Mom, the toy industry would be flatter than a Ken doll," says Palmer Gordon III, a securities analyst with Stanley Morgan in New York.

As it is, however, sales are as perky as Barbie. And that's not all. Traditionally, the toy industry has been highly cyclical, with Christmas accounting for about half of the year's sales. But Mattel Mom buys year-round—and may even splurge in summer, when her kids are home and she isn't. What's more, she doesn't flinch at the higher price points. "We estimate that the working mother spends $35.75 per toy, compared to a nonworking mother expenditure of $12.25," says Douglas Witherspoon, who follows the toy industry for Meryl Lunch.

To make sure they reach this market, toy manufacturers are taking unprecedented steps. It's not uncommon these days to see a full-page advertisement for Baby Wet-U2 ("With her own diaper service!") in *Business Week* and this newspaper. And companies are starting to develop toys that they believe have special appeal to the working mom:

- Taking a cue from Detroit, Mattel is re-engineering its best-selling Hot Wheels for what it perceives as a more conservative, safety-oriented buyer. Seat belts, left- and right-hand mirrors, and power steering are among the nonoptional extras.

- Hasbro is reportedly designing a G.I. Jane to sell alongside its ever-popular G.I. Joe. According to sources within the company, G.I. Jane is lean, mean and combat-ready, although, under Hasbro's policy, she may be deployed in military zones only to chauffeur G.I. Joe to the front line.

- Playskool, which makes a series of toys that allow the child to prepare "food" with Play-Doh, is becoming more nutrition-minded. Its new Sit-n-Eat line, to be introduced at the toy fair in New York this February, will include a "yogurt" maker, a "broccoli" steamer and even a breakfast kit that contains an "oatmeal" cooker.

- Aiming at the layette set, Fisher-Price has improved the technology of the "heartbeat"—an audio tape for newborns—to allow each working mother to record the sound of her own heart, skipped beats and all. The company is also doing R&D on a portable intercom that would allow a working mother to hear her baby cry within a ten-mile radius.

- For months, Mirage has had on the drawing board a reptilian heroine to add to its lineup of male Teenage Mutant Ninja Turtles. Product launch has been delayed indefinitely, however, while researchers try to identify a woman who painted during the Renaissance.

- WeeCare2, the nation's second largest day-care chain, has teamed up with several toy manufacturers to place small but well-stocked concessions at its centers across the nation. "Our hope is that the working mother may bribe her children to let her leave by giving them a new toy," a WeeCare2 executive explains.

The way the toy industry sees it, there's little danger it's investing too heavily in the working mother. "The more she works, the more she'll buy," says a spokesman for Toy Manufacturers of America, "and the more she buys, the more she'll need to work."

THE WORKING MOTHER'S GUIDE TO POPULAR TOYS

Most toy stores are so overstocked that it's hard to know what to buy. We understand how important it is that you get in and out of toy stores VERY QUICKLY. So, to protect your time, not to mention your sanity, we've looked at some popular toys and rated them for their guilt-reduction value to Working Mothers. Clip this guide and take it with you next time you venture into Toys Я Us.

Barbie—A fifties-style doll with breasts that defy gravity. DO NOT BUY. If you do, your little girl will start saying things like, "When I grow up I want to be beautiful like Barbie," thereby diminishing the possibility that—as the daughter of a Working Mother—she will develop more egalitarian views about gender.

Little Tikes Kitchen—A downsized, brightly colored replica of that dreary place you always seem to be cleaning. DO BUY. It may get your children accustomed to pitching in on household chores. To encourage this development, you may also consider purchasing a toy vacuum cleaner, an iron and ironing board, a mop, a broom, a small toilet brush, and (available in specialty shops only) a miniature washing machine and dryer.

Nintendo—A computer game that is seemingly more addictive than crack cocaine. DO BUY, despite several significant drawbacks, namely that microchip-generated sound will deplete both your sanity and the gray matter inside your child's skull. However, the down side must be weighed against a more pressing benefit: When you need a break from your kids, all you have to do is say, "Go play Nintendo" and they will not come back until they are twenty-one.

Teenage Mutant Ninja Turtles Paraphernalia—2.7 billion assorted objects ranging from cookie cutters and socks to small reptilian figures fashioned after characters created by two young guys in New Hampshire. DO NOT BUY on general principle alone: namely that no one, much less two guys in their twenties, should benefit so handsomely from one inane idea.

Baby Uh-Oh—A small, cuddly doll that actually produces poop in her diaper, thanks to space-age technology. DO BUY. In and of itself, this product has no intrinsic value, but that's just the point. The doll is so ridiculous that it will go out of production quickly. Then it will become rare. In the year 2050, it will command a high price from doll collectors, thus ensuring your granddaughter an inheritance that will allow her to choose whether or not to work when her children are young. (Note: Don't forget to save the dirty diapers.)

CHAPTER 18

Trying to Do It All

It's a well-established fact that Working Mothers have a compulsion to Do It All—everything their mothers did, everything their fathers did, and maybe a little bit more. Here, we provide documentation of how one Working Mother spends her time. Following is a typical day in the life of Karen Devaney:

9:00   Arrive at the office. Dash to Ladies' room to inspect for stains, apply eyeliner.

9:10   Marketing meeting to discuss latest sales trends for Crunchie Munchies.

9:11   Interrupt meeting to take urgent telephone call.
        Distraught day-care worker says Nora banged heads with another kid, blacked out and has been taken to emergency room.

9:30	Hospital. Doctor says Nora probably got angry and held her breath until she passed out. Drive her back to day-care, tell her to breathe.
10:30	Return to the office. Marketing meeting has just ended. Dash to Ladies' room to inspect for stains, repair makeup.
10:40	Take telephone call from reporter who says a scientist has found link between Crunchie Munchies and brain tumors. Assure him you'll have company response by noon.
10:45	Place phone call to scientist to check out brain tumor story. His line is busy. Leave a message asking him to return your call. Go pick up Josh for annual checkup by pediatrician.
11:15	Josh, in tears from shot for tetanus, calms down only with promise of french fries. Lunch at McDonald's.
12:15	Drop Josh at school and return to the office. Dash to Ladies' room to inspect for stains, repair makeup.
12:25	Phone reporter to ask for more time. His line is busy. Leave urgent message asking him to return your call.

12:30 Wire service runs story linking Crunchie Munchies to brain tumors.

12:31 GFC switchboard is flooded with calls. Stock plummets ten points. Boss heads out for drink to steady his nerves. Start updating résumé.

12:35 Josh's teacher calls to say that after-school center will be closed this afternoon for asbestos cleanup.

12:40 Call neighbor, a Stay-At-Home Mom, to ask if she can take Josh for the afternoon. Promise to make lemon meringue pie for school bake sale tomorrow.

1:00 Scientist returns your call. Seems he wasn't talking about brain tumors, but grain rumors—that Crunchie Munchie is developing a high-nutrition corn. Phone reporter.

1:10 Wire service runs correction.

1:11 Stock rises fifteen points. Boss congratulates you for fast work and heads out for drink to celebrate. Put away résumé, take out application for summer camp for Josh.

1:20 Telephone day-care center to see if Nora is still breathing. Teacher reminds you it's your turn to volunteer for field trip later in week.

1:30 Friend calls to suggest dinner this weekend. Start phoning around for baby-sitter.

2:40 Having found sitter, pick up Josh at school and deliver him to neighbor's. On way back to office, stop off at supermarket to buy lemons and at gas station for oil change. Mechanic says car needs complete overhaul.

3:40 Return to the office. Dash to credit union to ask about loan.

4:00 Meeting to discuss how to capitalize on favorable publicity for Crunchie Munchies.

4:01 Interrupt meeting to take telephone call from husband, who says he's working late tonight and you'll have to take Josh to Cub Scouts.

4:05 Return to meeting. Colleagues have just agreed GFC should undertake major new marketing campaign for Crunchie Munchies. Boss gives you one-week deadline.

4:55 Begin drafting new campaign.

5:00 Leave the office.

JUST SAY NO!

It's an old adage: "When you want something done, ask a busy person." That explains why the Working Mother is always recruited to serve as the class parent, host the soccer picnic, chair the PTA fund-raiser, organize the car pool.

By nature, you are inclined to oblige. Deep in your heart, you like to think you can Do It All.

Here's the Bad News: You Can't.

And here's the Good News: You Can Say No.

And here's the Even Better News. We're about to show you how.

Listed here are a variety of things you can say to get out of doing practically anything.

IF YOU WANT TO APPEAR...	SAY...
Diplomatic	I'm terribly sorry, but I've got a previous engagement.
Smooth	I'm tempted to say yes, but I think I'm going to have to pass this time.
Gracious	I'd be truly honored to, but this is a rather busy week (month, year, decade) for me and unfortunately, I won't be able to fit it in.
Subservient	I've got to check with my husband first, and he's out of town for the next two months.
Liberated	Why don't you ask my husband to do it?
Maternal	Any free time I have, I spend with my kids.
Theatrical	How absolutely marvelous of you to ask me! I'm completely devastated that I can't help out. (Exit laughing.)
Unequivocal	No way, José.
Childish	N-O. No! (For emphasis, stamp feet.)
Criminal	I'd be delighted. Not many places welcome ex-convicts as volunteers.
Deaf	SAY WHAT?

AN EXCERPT FROM THE *NATIONAL ENQUIRER*

OREGON WORKING MOM IS NINE WOMEN!

Bea Harris is one wacky gal. She's got nine personalities, and they all dote on her little boy!

Incredibly, Bea, 35, is also Sharon, Michele, Terry, Jennifer, Leslie, Lauren, Diane, Barbara and Joan. All nine of them live as one big happy family with Ken Harris, Bea's husband, and Ryan, their five-year-old son, in a mobile home in Portland, Oregon.

Bea has a syndrome known as Multiple Personality Disorder, or MPD, explained Dr. Herman Graf, a noted psychiatrist at the University of Bucharest. "Like the three faces of Eve, Bea has nine personalities that emerge at different times," he said. "The personalities, which even have different ages, can be called on as the need arises."

For example, Sharon, 42, is a hardworking nurse who brings home the bacon, while Michele is an exuberant 22-year-old who likes to play catch with Ryan and brainy Leslie, 32, helps him with his homework. Terry, 30, is a fanatical housekeeper. Diane, 38, the social gadabout in the group, goes to the PTA meetings.

Hubby Ken says he couldn't be happier. "We all get along together great and help each other out," he said. For Ryan, having nine moms is the most natural thing in the world, although he doesn't have much to say to Jennifer, the 18-year-old slut.

In fact, the only woman who says it isn't so great is Bea. "Sometimes I feel left out," she admitted. "I'm still looking for a personality of my own."

WORKING IT OUT

Working through the guilt. Maybe you thought that's what you do from nine to five, five days a week. But "working it through" is really psychobabble for understanding your guilt and—as they say—coming to terms with it. Below is a meeting between a Working Mother and the psychologist she consults about her guilt.

P: Perhaps you'd like to tell me why you're here.

WM: I came to see you because I feel guilty all the time, and I'd like to do something about it.

P: Why do you think you feel this way?

WM: Well, obviously—I should be with my kids more. But at work, I'm barely holding my own. And I don't give my husband the time he deserves. I'm not the perfect mother I thought I'd be.

P: You seem to think you're the only person who is able to take care of your children. That's the mark of a very narcissistic person.

WM: I never thought of myself as narcissistic. That's terrible. But after all, they are my kids. I should be spending more time with them.

P: You said should. Is that different from wanting to spend more time?

WM: I don't know. Maybe. I mean, I don't want to spend every minute with them, that's true. But it never occurred to me I don't want to be with them. . . . Now I feel really awful.

P: What about the other people in your life? How would you characterize your relationship with your husband?

WM: We still love each other, but it's kind of hard to be passionate in bed when the kids are in the next room. The last time we had sex, I kept thinking that what I really should be doing was making peanut butter and jelly sandwiches.

P: That's very interesting. What significance do you think peanut butter and jelly have for you?

WM: None. It's what the kids eat.

P: Perhaps we should talk about your work. How do you feel about your job?

WM: I used to like it a lot, but lately I feel that I'm just not giving it the attention it requires. I come in late and leave early and get almost nothing done in between.

P: Typical passive-aggressive behavior. (Glances at his watch.)

WM: Is it time for me to go? What do you mean, passive-aggressive?

P: We have another minute or two. It sounds like you're more than a little ambivalent toward your job. Perhaps what you're really trying to tell your boss is, "Fire me!"

WM: That's impossible! I need the money. And besides, you just said I don't want to be with my kids. . . . (Starts to cry.)

P: It seems to me you may be too easily influenced by other people's opinions of yourself. You need to work on developing a stronger sense of self-esteem.

WM: My self-esteem? But I've barely got time for my kids . . . or my husband . . . or my job. . . .

P: I'm sorry, our time is up. Perhaps you'd feel better if you made another appointment with me. Shall we say, the same time next week?

CHAPTER 19

Being Miserable

It's one of those days. Your kindergartner isn't talking to you because you picked him up late at school. Your baby has just swallowed your tax refund. The new project you hoped to work on went to your best friend—who, as your husband points out, is looking years younger than you. The forecast is for rain for the indefinite future.

Okay, you could be cheerful. You're a pro at being up when you're down. But why fight it? You're tired, frazzled, overworked, underpaid and guilty as all get-out. Let yourself go. Wallow in your misery. You've earned it.

To get you started, we've listed 101 things to be miserable about. But there's no need to stop here. Feel free to add your own.

101 THINGS TO BE MISERABLE ABOUT

1. Bubble gum stuck under the dining-room table
2. Play-Doh in your best sweater
3. Rainy weekends
4. Snot
5. That you didn't choose a more flexible career
6. That you didn't choose a better-paying career
7. That your best friend did
8. Disposable diapers that endanger the environment
9. Cloth diapers that endanger your sanity
10. "Leak-proof" diapers that leak
11. Poop
12. Overtime
13. The size of the child-care tax credit
14. Ear infectons
15. Insurance benefits for well-child care
16. VCR on the fritz
17. Apple juice
18. Braces
19. Breakfast meetings
20. Chuck E. Cheese
21. Adolescence
22. Puberty
23. Bambi's mother
24. Carsickness
25. Snow days

26. That your kid didn't start talking until he turned three
27. That he hasn't stopped talking since he turned three
28. My Little Pony
29. That you spend more on their shoes than on yours
30. That they need a new pair every two weeks
31. Dustballs
32. The size of your last raise

33. Your dress size
34. G.I. Joe
35. Laundry
36. That your new boss is five years younger than you
37. That your little girl wants a Barbie
38. That your little boy wants a gun
39. That your little boy doesn't want a gun
40. That your little boy wants a Barbie
41. Peter Pan's relationship with Wendy
42. The rule that two siblings never nap at the same time
43. School holidays
44. That you didn't get that promotion at work
45. That you got that promotion at work
46. Cinderella, Sleeping Beauty and Snow White as role models
47. Being called "poopy-head"
48. Deadlines
49. Winter
50. Summer
51. Head lice
52. The rented videotape you've had for seven days
53. Bubble gum in the VCR
54. The Teenage Mutant Ninja Turtles
55. The teenage mutant baby-sitter who didn't show up Saturday night
56. That your child's school recycles but you don't
57. Your daughter's phone call to the office (fifth today)
58. The kitchen floor
59. The pony at a classmate's birthday party
60. Birthday parties in general
61. Happy Meals
62. The bottom of the toybox
63. Peer pressure, theirs

64. Peer pressure, yours
65. Toys Я Us
66. That you haven't seen this year's Oscar winners
67. That you never even heard of them
68. The hours between 5:30 and 7:30 P.M.
69. The Consumer Price Index
70. Jim Henson's untimely death
71. That you can't stop whistling "Itsy Bitsy Spider"
72. That your son just learned to whistle
73. Designer infant wear
74. Nintendo

75. Teenage sex
76. The missing mitten
77. Amoxicillin
78. Whining
79. Honey in your daughter's hair
80. Perfect Mothers
81. That you missed the deadline for summer camp
82. Odd socks
83. Night terrors
84. Your friend who never gives her kids hot dogs
85. The back seat of your car
86. The Hurried Child
87. Your performance review
88. Sugary cereals

89. Separation anxiety
90. That you forgot your godchild's birthday
91. Strep throat
92. Extended business trips
93. Banana stains
94. Saturday at the supermarket
95. 2 A.M. feedings
96. $40 T-shirts
97. Teacher training days
98. That you didn't have kids when you were younger
99. That you didn't wait until you were older to have kids
100. That they're clingy for so long
101. That they grow up so fast

CHAPTER 20

Focusing on the Bright Side, Which May Not Be So Ridiculous After All

Okay, okay, enough bitching and moaning. Deep in your heart, you know that being a Working Mother isn't all that awful. In fact, when you consider the alternatives—not working or not being a mother—it's positively wonderful.

Sometimes, though, the reality gets buried in the chaos of everyday life. When that happens, force yourself to look on the bright side. Even though you might not be Doing It All, you're Doing an Awful Lot.

To keep things in perspective, we suggest you carry this book with you at all times. When life gets frenzied and the pace gets hectic, take a few minutes out and turn to this page. It will make you feel better. Honest.

PASTE YOUR FAVORITE PICTURES OF YOUR SMILING CHILDREN HERE.

PASTE YOUR FAVORITE PICTURES OF YOUR SMILING CHILDREN HERE.

PASTE YOUR FAVORITE PICTURES OF YOUR SMILING CHILDREN HERE.

PASTE YOUR FAVORITE PICTURES OF YOUR SMILING CHILDREN HERE.

PASTE YOUR FAVORITE PICTURES OF YOUR SMILING CHILDREN HERE.

PASTE YOUR FAVORITE PICTURES OF YOUR SMILING CHILDREN HERE.

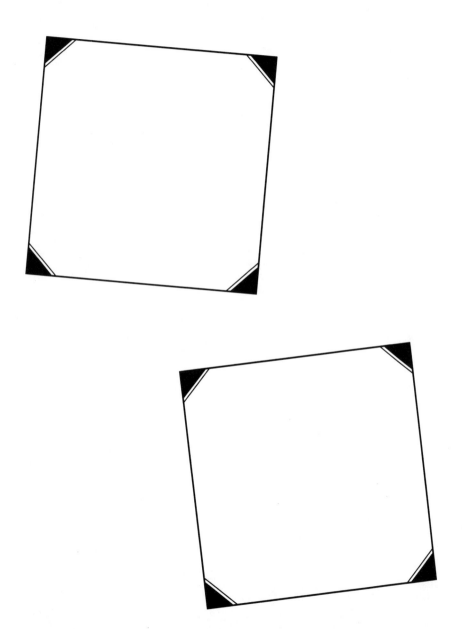